Worthless

The Young Person's Indispensable Guide to Choosing the Right Major

Aaron Clarey

Published by Paric Publishing

ISBN: 1467978302
ISBN-13: 978-1467978309

To Varmint

TABLE OF CONTENTS

CHAPTER 1
LUCKY YOU

"I Don't Care About Your Feelings, I Care About You."

You are lucky. And the reason you are lucky is because somebody cares enough about you and your future to have given you this book. Oh, sure, at first it may not seem like a huge or caring gesture.

"A book, yippee!!! Just what I always wanted!"

But what you don't realize is the courage it took for that person to buy you this book.

This book isn't a "touchy feel good" book. It isn't a book about finding yourself. It's not a romance book where "vampires" protect their human female love interest from Ebola-infected "wolfmen." And it's not one of those lame self-help books like "Find Your Inner You" or "Yea for Us, We're All Winners." It's a cold, harsh, blunt book that delivers the strongest belt of reality you'll ever have. A much-needed belt of reality. A belt of reality so harsh and blunt that it may even offend you and make you upset at the person who bought you this book. However, that's precisely why you must appreciate that person.

Understand it takes nothing to say nice things to nice people. The average person could go all day paying compliments and platitudes, giving everybody warm fuzzies in their stomachs. There's no risk and there's no (immediate) drawback. But what takes real guts and real tough, fatherly love is to tell somebody the truth. No matter how much they don't want to hear it. No matter how much it may hurt their "feelings." And no matter how much it may risk their friendship or relationship, telling the truth is the ultimate sign of somebody who genuinely cares about you because, frankly...

the truth is not optional.

Understand, no matter how much you may not like "the truth," the truth is the truth. It's reality. It cannot be avoided.

Oh, sure you can lie to yourself and tell yourself what you want to hear. And oh, sure, you can rationalize reality away with warped and unrealistic thinking. And oh, sure, there's no limit to the number of people who will gladly tell you what you want to hear because they'll profit from it at your expense.

You can live in La-La Land for quite some time.

But ultimately, in the end, reality wins. And if you've lived your life ignoring reality because you simply "didn't like it" or because your environment was programmed to tell you what you wanted to hear, you will suffer great and unimaginable consequences. Conversely, if you lived in reality and made your decisions based in the real world, you will reap great and unimaginable benefits. And that is the aim of this book:

To make sure you make one of the most important decisions in your life based in reality and not your feelings.

One Hell of a Decision

You are about to make a decision that will affect your future more significantly than any other decision you have made thus far. It will determine how much money you make, what kind of standard of living you will enjoy, how healthy you will be, how healthy your children will be, and what you will do with the majority of your adult time.

You will inevitably work eight hours a day for 30-40 years. This will be, hands down, the single biggest plurality of your conscious time on this planet. It will not be spent with your loving husband or wife. It will not be spent with your future children or dogs. It will not be spent drinking margaritas on a beach or playing video games. It will be spent working for somebody else. How enjoyable and rewarding all of this will be boils down to one simple decision – what are you going to major in?

Naturally, such a decision should not be made lightly, nor should it be made in haste. You should spend a lot of time thinking about it, studying and researching various majors, and doing whatever you can to come to a wise decision. But for all the importance associated with this decision, and the huge effect it will have on your life, the truth is most young people receive little to no help or guidance in making this decision from their elders. It is the epitome of irony that you have this monstrously huge and important decision to make, and yet nobody, be it your parents, your guidance counselors, or your teachers, can provide you with any real, concrete help and insight as to what you should choose as your future profession. This relegates most young people to make this daunting decision on their own who do not have the experience, background, or wisdom to choose a major wisely.

Making matters worse, there are "adults" out there who have no problem taking advantage of young people like you and your situation. They'll tell you what you want to hear, cajole or convince you to attend a certain school, or pursue a certain study simply because they will profit from it. There are entire industries based on convincing you to spend your education dollars on them, while effectively offering nothing in return. And perhaps most despicably, there are politicians, special interest groups, unions and lobbyists who have no moral qualms about using you and other fellow innocent youths as pawns to advance their political aims and agendas.

Thus, the reason for this book.

"Worthless" will help you navigate this minefield and choose the major that is right for you. It will explain to you how the labor market works, why some professions make more than others, review starting salaries and explore different options when it comes to undergrad and grad school.

It will also show you how different people in society prey upon youth, such as yourself, and take advantage of you for their own personal gain so that you can identify these threats and avoid them. But ultimately, however, this book is nothing more than the wisdom of your elders who have gone down this path before, who want you to learn from our mistakes so that you might have a better, easier and happier life than we did.

CHAPTER 2
BASIC ECONOMICS

Below are excerpts from several articles during "The Great Recession." There is a common thread that is blindingly obvious to any adult that has ever searched for a job, but it may not be blindingly obvious to you. Read through them and see if you can identify what all five of these people have in common.

From "Oregonlive.com," June 12th, 2010;

After a yearlong search, Jackie Mroz, 22, of Oregon City, is about to get some experience, but at a cost.

She put everything she had into her studies at the University of Oregon, graduating in 2009 with degrees in international studies and sociology and a double minor in nonprofit administration and African studies. She studied abroad in Senegal, took challenging courses, earned a 3.8 grade point average and raced through college in three years.

"It has gotten me pretty much nowhere," she said.

When she graduated, Mroz figured she would quickly land a job with an international nonprofit. After two months, she took on a catering job as she broadened her search. Still living with her parents in Oregon City, she sent out more than 70 carefully prepared job applications and resumes.

"I never got a single interview, except for the catering company," she said...

"I have gone through weeks when I completely doubted myself," she said. "What am I doing wrong? It is a question I ask everyday. ....After a year of getting basically no response, you start giving up."

From the same article;

Audra Armen-Van Horn, 23, Portland, worked for Victoria's Secret while earning her psychology degree from the University of Oregon. Now, a year after graduating in 2009 and applying for more than 100 jobs, she's still working part time for the store while hoping to get a job with the American Cancer Society.

"I have a bachelor's degree, and I'm making $8.50 an hour," she said. "It is pretty depressing..."

Also from the same article;

Mindy Lary, 27, Beaverton, can testify to that. She graduated in 2009 with a Master of Art in elementary school teaching from the University of Portland and has been substitute teaching since.

"I applied for 75 teaching jobs, anything within an hour's drive of the Portland area, and I didn't even get an interview," she said.

From "The Dartmouth," November 4th, 2011

Frank, who majored in English, said he was surprised by the economic realities he faced after graduation.

"No one told us that it was going to be hard," he said. "No one told us we couldn't get a job until we didn't get jobs. People a little older than me got their dream jobs like they were supposed to, and then were fired when the crisis hit."...

Frank faced much difficulty in his job search and initially accepted an internship in the artistic department of the Public Theater in New York City. Although he did receive a small stipend, he lived at home for the length of the internship because he couldn't afford rent, or even "enough food for the week," he said.

From "The Huffington Post," November 3rd, 2011;

Recent college graduate Molly Katchpole has $2,200 to her name, holds down two part-time jobs – one of them as a nanny – and describes her financial situation as paycheck to paycheck. So when Bank of America announced that it would begin charging debit card users a $5 monthly fee, Katchpole got mad and started an online petition. More than 300,000 people signed it...

Bottom of FormKatchpole grew up in Cumberland, R.I., a town of 33,000, and graduated last spring from Roger Williams University in Bristol, R.I., with a degree in art and architectural history. She was on the debate team in high school and wrote letters to her local paper...

She and her boyfriend live in a tiny, one-bedroom basement apartment, where they split the $1,250 rent. Sisko works as a paralegal, and Katchpole is hoping to find a full-time job in politics.

From "The Nation," November 2, 2011;

A few years ago, Joe Therrien, a graduate of the NYC Teaching Fellows program, was working as a full-time drama teacher at a public elementary school in New York City. Frustrated by huge class sizes, sparse resources and a disorganized bureaucracy, he set off to the University of Connecticut to get an MFA in his passion—puppetry. Three years and $35,000 in student loans later, he emerged with degree in hand, and because puppeteers aren't exactly in high demand, he went looking for work *at his old school… even though Joe's old principal was excited to have him back, she just couldn't afford to hire a new full-time teacher. Instead, he's working at his old school as a full-time "substitute"; he writes his own curriculum, holds regular classes and does everything a normal teacher does. "But sub pay is about 50 percent of a full-time salaried position," he says, "so I'm working for half as much as I did four years ago, before grad school, and I don't have health insurance…. It's the best-paying job I could find."*

Now there are many things these people have in common. They can't find jobs. They all graduated from college. Some of you may have even been savvy enough to notice they all theme or center around kind of an "artsy fartsy," non-profit, government type theme (which will prove relevant later, but not for this particular point). But, what they ultimately have in common is one thing:

They all have worthless degrees.

"International Studies," "Sociology," "Non-profit Administration," "African Studies," "English," "Psychology," "Elementary Education," "Art and Architectural History," and, of course my personal favorite, a "Masters in Puppetry."

All degrees, all worthless.

And the reason they are worthless is because of one simple thing:

There just isn't any demand for them.

Certainly, some of them may be rewarding intellectually. Certainly, studying these subjects might prove interesting or fun. But ultimately, in the end, they have no economic worth. They are in the financial sense LITERALLY "worthless."

Now normally when you ask a person why they chose a worthless major, they get all defensive, tighten up and give you the standard knee-jerk response:

"Well, it's not all about the money! I did it for intellectual purposes!"

And that's all fine and well.

But what is particularly interesting to note is how some of the people highlighted in the above articles are "shocked" or "surprised" or even depressed they couldn't find jobs. It's as if they thought they could just pick any ol' major and expect employment. Not only does this show you they really were doing it for the money, but it also behooves the questions:

How did they ever come to think this kind of degree would help them make money?

Who on god's green Earth led them to believe these degrees would end up with them making $90,000 plus a $20,000 signing bonus?

What did you expect with a MASTERS in PUPPETRY???

However, this difference between what they were expecting and what reality inevitably dished out to them belies something else was going on. That they were either spectacularly ignorant about the realities of what their degrees would do for them or they were purposely misled about it. The truth is (as you'll come to find out) it was a combination of both. These kids were both ignorant about what their degrees could do for them, and they were also actively misled.

Being actively misled about something, especially by your elders or people you thought you could trust, is one thing. It's not their fault nobody stepped in to tell them,

"Hey, that degree in 'African Studies' isn't worth the $80,000 in student debt you're going to incur."

So in that regard being misled is quite forgivable. However, what is not forgivable is the ignorance these people had when they chose a major. Specifically, an ignorance of basic economics which plagues not just most youth today, but most adults as well. And it is here that we must focus our studies because it is economics that fundamentally governs the labor market and consequently how much money you make based on what major you choose.

Economics Lesson #1 - Joe Mauer and the School Teacher

No matter what your teachers and mentors told you, no matter what your parents or people older than you said, and no matter what your guidance counselor told you, the major you choose and the commensurate success that comes with it boils down to two simple things:

Supply and demand.

That's it. No more, no less. It really cannot get any simpler than that.

Supply and demand.

Any attempts or efforts to make it more complicated than that is simply somebody trying to lie to you. It doesn't matter "if you follow your heart." It doesn't matter if your employer practices "corporate social responsibility." It doesn't matter if you "go green" or "recycle." And it doesn't matter if you have on your resume that you donated time helping the endangered "Oogoo Boogoo" tribe.

What will ultimately determine your paycheck at the end of the day is supply and demand.

"Supply and demand for what?" you might ask.

Supply and demand for your skills.

And nothing exemplifies this point better than comparing two very different types of people with two very different types of skills - Joe Mauer (a professional baseball player) and your average elementary school teacher.

Normally when you hear about professional athletes and teachers it's usually in the context of how "unfair" it is that Joe Mauer makes $580 billion dollars and the poor elementary school teacher only makes $3.46 a decade. The natural human inclination is to abandon thought and replace it with feelings and emotion and side with the teacher. Naturally educating children is more important than seeing some guy swing a stick and hit a sphere over a fence. But what most people don't realize is that they made a vital mistake when analyzing this situation. They let their emotions or what they'd "like" to see happen overrule reality.

Understand economics is not compassionate. It doesn't have feelings. It isn't sentient. It doesn't care. Economics is reality. It is what it is. It doesn't matter what you would "like." It doesn't matter what teachers would “like.” It only matters what the majority of people with the majority of dollars would like. And the majority of people would rather pay $50 a ticket to see Joe Mauer swing a stick at a sphere than the average kid being forced to go to yet another boring day of school in the 4th grade. It may not be “right,” it may not be “moral,” but morality and idealism are irrelevant because reality trumps both.

The harshness of economic reality does not stop there. We’ve only thus far addressed the demand side of the equation and concluded (rightly so) that there is more demand for watching baseball than there is going to school. What we have yet to address is supply.

Of the seven billion people on the planet there are maybe a couple hundred that can hit a home run. And of that couple hundred, even fewer can keep a batting average of above .300. But of the seven billion people on the planet, nearly all of them could become teachers. The reason why is that it’s easy to become a teacher. The skills are not unique. It doesn’t take an incredible amount of intelligence or skill. Pretty much anybody can get their degree in education. But very few of us can hit a ball like Joe Mauer.

In other words the supply of Joe Mauer’s is very limited, whereas the supply of teachers is nearly infinite. There are literally MILLIONS of education majors and there is only one Joe Mauer. So, naturally when you have millions of people all willingly forking over $50 each to see Joe Mauer, he and other professional athletes are going to make many times more than the average teacher. Not because they are mean or greedy, nor is it because the teachers are inept and don't deserve a paycheck. It just simply boils down to the fact that there is a flood of teachers in the labor market and maybe 300 outstanding baseball players.

Now of course we all can't become professional baseball players, but it is not an issue of developing a rare skill such as hitting home runs in the major leagues. It's a matter of finding professions or majors where the supply of those professionals is small or limited while the demand for their services is high. Professions such as surgeons, CPA's, petroleum engineers, physicians, computer network engineers, etc. Professions that are by no means easy, but by all means infinitely more possible than becoming the next Joe Mauer.

Economics Lesson #2 – It DOES Take a Village

Economics has the reputation for being boring. This is primarily due to the fact that economics is usually taught by economists and economists are not known for their charm, charisma or ability to attract the ladies. Regardless, the end result is the majority of the population is not only indifferent about economics, but they have an incredibly poor grasp of it. Worse still is economics gets the reputation of being "complex" or "difficult" to understand when in reality that could not be further from the truth. So when I first started teaching economics in college I came up with a rather simple concept that helped explain economics in a very clear and simple manner which to this day I believe is still the single best way to explain it. That concept is "The Village."

Imagine if you would a medieval village in Europe in the 1100's. Back then the continent was largely comprised of individual villages, secluded and sectioned off from any major towns or metropolises. Because they were standalone villages, the people in that town were completely dependent upon themselves to provide for themselves. No outside help or support would be provided to them.

This necessitated each village be self-supporting and self-sustaining. And, if you looked at 1100's Europe, you would see that the types of jobs and professions the villagers took on reflected this fact. You had the butcher, the farmer, the blacksmith, the clothier, the knight, the baker, the goldsmith and of course the all-important grog maker. Everybody had a job or a task that carried their weight in the village. What you did NOT have was the professional activist, the social worker, the starving artist, the trophy wife, the socialite or the village welfare bum. Everybody had a job and everybody's job provided vital and required services and products to the village.

Now, the reason we understand this is because a village is a small enough entity for us to wrap our brains around. We see the little village with the little cows and the village people walking in the muddy streets. But ask yourself this question:

How is a country any different than a village?

Is not a country a self-contained economic entity just like a village? Is not a country nothing more than an amalgamation of people working to support themselves? Sure a country has a lot more people and may cover a wider area, but in the end a country is just a really big village. And just like our friends in the 1100 medieval European village, the citizens of countries today must produce something of value or else the country perishes.

Of course, with countries being much larger and more populous than villages, as well as the fact through technology and innovation we've been able to create so much wealth a lot of people don't have to work. But that still doesn't change the fundamental fact that in order to survive and progress the people of the "village" as a whole must produce something of value. The more specific and moral question is do you carry your own weight in this village? Do you produce something of value OTHER PEOPLE WANT? Something that is of service or in demand. Not something you "want" to produce and to hell with the rest of the village if they don't pay you for it.

When you ask yourself this question, "What do people in our modern day village want?" you will start to see more clearly what fields of study are the ones that pay.

Economics Lesson #3 – Your Christmas Wish List

Baseball professionals and medieval European villages aside, probably the single best thing I can do to convey to you the importance of choosing the right major is a little exercise I had my students go through. I took all the students and had them list the top 5 things they wanted to buy or planned on buying in the near future. It could be anything, gas, video games, food, you name it. You yourself could do the same right now, list the top five things you want to buy or are planning on buying in the near future. The lists that were typically compiled in class looked something like this:

Gasoline
Video Games
Clothes
Sports Car
Motorcycle
Cigarettes
Smart Phone/MP3 Player
New Phone

Booze/Beer
Flat Screen TV/LCD
Sushi
Jewelry
Computer
Moped
Trip Overseas
Movies (DVD's)
Stereo System

The next thing I would have my students do is list their majors, and invariably I would end up with a list like this (repeat majors exist because there was more than one person majoring in that field):

Sociology
Women's-Studies
Accounting
Journalism
Engineering
Psychology
Education
Psychology
Pre-Law
Psychology
Actuarial Science
Communications
Political Science
International Relations
Journalism

Accounting
Sociology
Music/Arts
African American Studies
Pre-Med
Political Science
History
Education
History

The two lists by themselves had nothing obvious or noteworthy about them. However, when you compared them side to side you could see a problem:

Gasoline	Sociology
Video Games	Women's Studies
Clothes	Electrical Engineering
Sports Car	Journalism
Motorcycle	Engineering
Cigarettes	English
Phone/MP3 Player	Psychology
New Phone	Education
Cell Phone Bill	Pre-Law
Booze/Beer	Psychology
Flat Screen TV/LCD	Actuarial Science
Sushi	Communications
Shoes	Political Science
Utilities	International Relations
Jewelry	Journalism
Computer	Accounting

Moped
Trip to Overseas
Movies (DVD's)
Tuition
Stereo System
Rent

Philosophy
Sociology
Music/Arts
African American Studies
Pre-Med
Political Science
History
Education

In short, there was a huge mismatch between what people wanted and what they were studying. Everybody wanted cars, MP3 players, motorcycles and gas, but nobody was willing to study the fields that ultimately produced these items. Nobody was studying what would be necessary to create an MP3 player or build a car. Everybody wanted gas, but not one petroleum engineer was in the group. And nearly everybody wanted a huge flat panel TV, presumably on the assumption the ONE electrical engineering major would charitably make a score of flat panel TV's for everybody else.

Also ironic was how there were so many sociology majors, but not one person listed "social work" in their wish list. There was always the token women's studies major, but I have yet to see a student ask Santa for a "A lecture about women's studies." Also was the token English major, but oddly enough everybody in my class already spoke, read and wrote English quite fluently.

There was also no shortage of psychology majors, but not one person ever listed "therapy" on their wish list.

This mismatch between what people want and the skilled labor required to build it makes it very clear the problem facing youth today. You all want to have high paying jobs, you all want to go to college, but you never give an ounce of thought as to what is in demand. Most youth today major in what they WANT, not what other people DEMAND. This not only goes a long way in explaining why liberal art majors face high unemployment and low-paying jobs, but also explains why we have a trade deficit with the likes of China and India whose students DO major in the fields that produce the goods we want.

Economics Lesson #4 – Starting Salaries

We can talk about the mismatch of skills being learned versus the products we demand or the eccentricities of the professional sports labor market all we want, but inevitably the economics of choosing the right major boils down to one simple thing – starting salaries.

You don't have to get your doctorate in economics with a specialization in labor market economics to understand this. The labor market makes it very easy to identify which majors are most in demand and this is reflected numerically in starting salaries or average wages. You'll note the fields that pay the most are (surprise surprise) the fields that produce the stuff you want. Engineering, computer programming, chemistry, accounting, etc. etc. You'll also notice some majors, such as accounting, that are higher-paying, but you can't see an obvious connection between an accountant and how they would make MP3 players. Keep in mind electrical engineers alone cannot make MP3 players. You need a company, a company that employs, among other things, accountants, executives, chemists, purchasers, managers, engineers, actuaries and so forth. So it is not just the fields that are directly related to the production of in-demand goods and services. It's any field that also supports the production of those goods.

2009 Starting Salaries (Source: NACE)

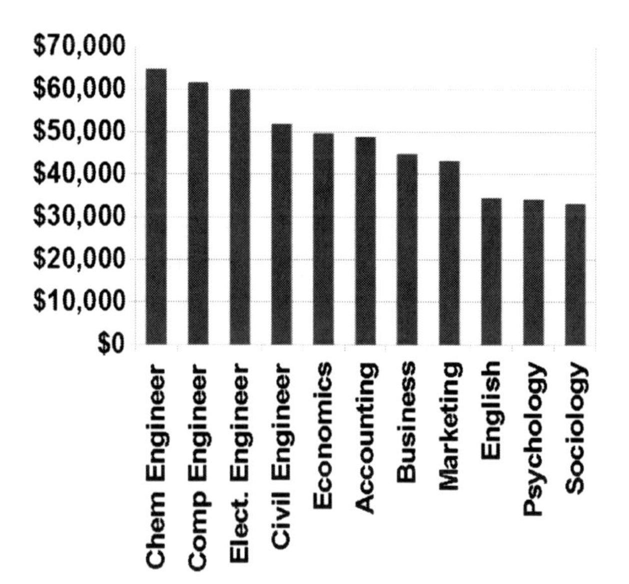

Essentially, this is all you really need to govern your decision about which fields to consider majoring in. Of course starting salaries should not be the only thing you use to make your decision. You would obviously like to choose a field that you have an interest in. But if you are going to spend 4-5 years of your youth pursuing a degree, not to mention tens of thousands of dollars, the financial return on this investment must be considered.

CHAPTER 3
WHAT TO STUDY

"Embrace the Math, Love the Math! The Math is Your Friend!"

With a solid review of the economics behind the labor market we already have a pretty good idea of what to study. But to put it even more succinctly, you want to major in what is called "STEM."

STEM stands for:

Science
Technology
Engineering and
Math

Majors that fall under "STEM" are typically those that are the highest paying. If you remember the chart from chapter two, you saw that engineers, computer programmers, etc., were the ones who had the highest starting salaries. You may also have noticed majors such as accounting, economics or statistics were also reasonably highly ranked. Regardless of the major, the one thread they have in common is that they all involve math.

Yes, math.

I know at this point most people have probably tuned out. They didn't like math in school. They probably weren't very good at math. And for the most part, people just plain don't like math.

To that I respond with one simple word;

"Tough."

The reason I say, "tough" is not to be mean, but because there is something much more fundamental about math. Realize saying, "Well, I don't like math," is like saying, "Well, I don't like gravity," or "I don't like the sun rising in the east," or "I don't like wet water."

Math is math.

It's reality. And whether you enjoy math or not doesn't matter.

Furthermore, the economic REALITY of the situation is that if you want to make a decent living, you have to learn math. There are no ifs, ands, or buts about it. Math is not optional.

There is good news, however. Despite what some people will say, one's mathematical ability is not dependent on some sort of "aptitude" or "natural skill." It's not dependent on your "gender" or upbringing. It's really more of a function of how much effort you've put into it. The reason why is that math is finite. It is logical. It always follows set precise rules. It always has set precise answers. I loved math in school not because I had any penchant for it, but because unlike English or History where if the teacher simply didn't like you they could mark you down for some lame excuse or another, math you either got the problem right or you didn't no matter how much your teacher hated you.

Regardless, yes, math can get complex, but it is completely understandable by the average human brain. It's whether the human with the brain can turn off the reality TV show, or set down the video game controller, and focus their efforts towards learning math. So, do not be deterred or frightened just because a subject requires a lot of math. Matter of fact, you should embrace the math. Accept the math. Learn to love the math. The math is your friend. The math shall set you free. Because, ultimately, it is through math you will achieve financial stability and an increased chance of life-long happiness.

Not All STEMS Were Created Equal

Understand, however, that it is not just a simple matter of mastering linear calculus and POOF! You'll get a job offer of $120,000 a year, plus bonus. Math merely gives you the raw talent that can be further honed and specialized into a practical, employable skill. And though all STEM majors require a significant amount of math, not all of them result in high paying jobs. Therefore, we will look at various STEM majors in terms of their employability and earnings potential as well as highlight some of the STEM majors that are not as lucrative.

Your most profitable STEM degrees are those that not only have math, but then have another highly skilled component, notably chemistry. It is no coincidence that petroleum and chemical engineers make the most money. They not only have to master all the physics and math that go into traditional engineering, they must also master the world of chemistry and alloys and polymers. Most petroleum engineers take more than four years to graduate, but they make more than any of their other engineering counterparts.

Ranked right below chemical engineers are electrical or computer engineers. These engineers, just like petroleum or chemical engineers, must also major in a second discipline outside engineering and that is electricity. But again, we see the value of mastering and combining two subjects. Computer engineers create, among many other things, your computers, processors, MP3 players, phones, and other electrical devices you rely upon every day. Because of this, they command the second-highest salaries in the engineering fields.

Below these specialized engineering fields comes mechanical engineering or just "engineering." Certainly not easy by any means, but in general "mechanical engineers" are more plentiful, and not as specialized as your petroleum or electrical engineers. However, engineers are in demand and because of this they still command a much higher salary than your average liberal arts major.

Finally, there is "civil engineering." These are people who design civil projects such as sewer systems, bridges, roads and so forth. It is not as specialized as the other fields of engineering, and other engineers will often joke or mock "civil engineers" about not being "real engineers." However, this is largely professional joking and though civil engineers are typically at the bottom when it comes to earnings potential of all the engineering fields, it still commands a decent salary.

Now, these aforementioned fields of engineering are all worthwhile STEM degrees. They ultimately produce something of value, they command high wages, and if you get a degree in any one of those fields, employment should not be too much of a problem in your future. However, there are other legitimate engineering majors that require just as much math and just as much effort as those mentioned above, but due to economic factors do not command as high of salaries.

A perfect example is nuclear engineering. Most people would think nuclear engineers would be in very high demand. However, since political forces are moving away from nuclear power and more towards wind, coal, and natural gas, ironically one of the harder engineering majors has little demand in the labor market. Of course this could change if all of the sudden energy policy favored building new nuclear power plants, but in today's current energy labor market, the demand for nuclear engineers is not as high as it is for say an electrical engineer (though there are some people in foreign countries who may appreciate your services).

Very similar to nuclear engineering is aerospace engineering. This major in particular snatches some young boys from the other engineering fields because as boys grow up they find fighter planes, space exploration and flight very interesting. Sadly because of the interest, not only are aerospace programs flooded with more majors than what the labor market typically calls for, the aerospace industry is also heavily influenced by the economy, as well as military spending. Say it was the 1980's when then President Reagan was building up the military and the economy was booming. Demand for aerospace engineers was very high, not just to build commercial planes for airlines, but to build new fighter planes to help fight the Cold War. However, when communism fell in 1991 the demand for fighter planes and military spending dropped, bringing demand for new aerospace engineers down with it.

While it seems I'm ragging on aerospace and nuclear engineering, keep in mind you could do a lot worse. The average nuclear engineer and average aerospace engineer certainly make more money than your average accountant and certainly more than your average teacher. However, it is the volatility of the market for these majors that I am trying to warn you about. Besides, there are much worse engineering degrees you could waste your youth and your money on, most notably "Architecture" and "Environmental Engineering."

"Architecture" is probably the most worthless engineering degree there is. Mock civil engineering all you want, Architecture is the lazy man's way to an engineering degree. It is not as mathematically rigorous as your average engineering major, it's not as practical as your average engineering major, but worse still are the realities of the architecture labor market.

Everybody wants to be an "architect."

"Ooo! Look at me!!! I design pretty buildings!! Yeaaa for me!!!"

That's pretty much what every naive 17 year old thinks when they decide they'll become an architect. However, for every young idealistic boy or girl who thinks it would be fun to design buildings, they have to realize there are 20 or 30 more other 17 year old boys and girls that have the exact same diabolical plan.

This results in the most over-supplied labor market of all the engineering fields. So over-supplied that if you want to become an actual architect nearly all of the states require you get a license to do so, and in order to get a license you need your DOCTORATE in Architecture (except in Arizona). Of course by the time you're done getting your doctorate in anything, your mind will have been so numbed it will have lost any genuine creativity it may have once had in its youth (which also goes a long way in explaining why modern day architecture for the most part sucks).

But, the question is whether you have the time or the money to pursue what is essentially a very expensive hobby. You'll find, if you look at a lot of architects, they come from rich families that could afford to put their child through college for 9-10 years and already had a job lined up for them through familial connections. Unless you have rich parents and don't need to worry about money, do not pursue architecture as a career.

As bad as Architecture is as a major, there is another engineering major that is equally worthless.

"Environmental Engineering."

The sad, cold, harsh truth is that environmental engineering really isn't a legitimate field of study. The reason it exists is in response to the political environmental movement that started in the late 1960's. No doubt, just like me when I was your age, you have been bombarded about various environmental issues such as global warming, going green, and recycling in school. Back in our day it was "the ozone layer," "nuclear waste," "acid rain," and "the rain forests." It really doesn't matter what the "cause of the day" is because they are all politically motivated and not causes that are based in reality. But, just because something isn't based in reality, doesn't mean it will stop people with political motivations.

Understand there was no demand for environmental engineers back in the 1960's, and there really isn't any demand now. So why do environmental engineering programs exist? Because with millions of young people being told everyday about the importance of the environment for the past 40 years, a demand to major in something environmentally-based evolved.

Re-read that last sentence because it's very important;

" Because with millions of young people being told everyday about the importance of the environment for the past 40 years, ***a demand to major in something environmentally based evolved.***"

In other words, they have it mixed up. They have it reversed. No firms or employers demanded environmental engineers. It wasn't like there was a shift in the economy that caused business to start employing millions of youth as environmental engineers. It was the youth (prompted by their elders) who decided they wanted to major in something in response to all the environmentalist propaganda they received in school, not the real-world economic demands of the labor market. Once again, you see this is like living in the village and telling the villagers you're going to study art and they better pay you for it whether they want to or not.

However, this "cart before the horse" analogy, though accurate, is not the primary reason to avoid majoring in Environmental Engineering. The primary reason is actually quite simple - look at any of the renewable energy sources and technologies and what kinds of engineers are hired to produce them.

If you look at wind turbines they don't hire "environmental engineers" to build them. They employ:

Mechanical engineers,
Electrical engineers, and
Aerospace engineers.

If you look at solar panels, they don't hire "environmental engineers" to build them. They employ:

Electrical engineers,
Chemical engineers, and
Mechanical engineers.

In other words, "Environmental Engineering" didn't evolve in response to a demand for it in the labor market. It evolved because people wanted to major in it in the hopes there would be demand for their services. Demand that just simply doesn't exist for jobs being done by other engineers.

"Is There A Doctor in the House?"

Again, like engineering, you might think just because a subject is in the bio-sciences and is therefore "STEM" then it's guaranteed you're going to get a good job. However bio-sciences also has its fair share of worthwhile and worthless degrees.

Obviously dental, medical and surgical degrees and thus Pre-Med as a major is a wise choice. It takes a very long time to get your MD or DDS, but when you do, you pretty much don't have to worry about employment for the rest of your life. I personally wish I could have become a doctor, but beyond the 10 years of schooling it would take, a major drawback is having to be able to cut somebody open and not pass out. This is actually quite a legitimate reason not to become a doctor.

Nursing is an outstanding field where you can make a lot of money, especially if you specialize in a particular field (surgical nurse, anesthesiology, etc.). Again, though, you may have to witness or participate in "The Cutting of the People Open," which is again one of the few legitimate reasons not to major in something. However, there are some other good and great fields in the bio-sciences that don't necessarily involve bloodshed.

Pharmacy is a great field to get into. You do of course need extensive studying in chemistry and biology, and for all practical purposes you will study just as much as you would to become a doctor. You will inevitably need six additional years of schooling beyond your bachelors and have to pass a certification exam for the state, but in the end you will be making at least $70,000 and also never have to worry about employment.

Related to pharmacy are pharmaceuticals. Multi-billion dollar companies that make multi-billion dollar profits every year by creating and developing new drugs. Any field here that results in the development and creation of new life-saving drugs is also in high demand. Fields such as chemistry, bio-chemistry, virology and bio-engineering.

However, nestled within the bio-sciences are two majors that can be considered pretty worthless. Those majors are "Biology" and "Kinesiology."

Biology, unto itself may not seem like a worthless major, and technically it isn't. However, the bio-sciences field is unique in that it deals with such a wide-array of health issues and, more importantly, your subjects are human. Because of this, a simple degree in biology is not honed or refined enough to help advance all the various and many specialized sub-studies of the bio-sciences field. Furthermore, since you will ultimately be working on other human beings, to become employed in the field you'll need a lot of schooling beyond a bachelors to ensure, quite simply, you don't hurt or kill anybody else.

Therefore, for the most part, those with a stand-alone biology degree really can't do much beyond going to the local high school and teaching. You can teach the basics of biology to high school kids and if you screw up with the scalpel the worst thing you'll hurt is a frog or a worm. But if you really have a passion for the bio-sciences the biology degree will simply be a required stepping stone to achieving something greater.

While biology does have merit, the same cannot be said for "Kinesiology." The reason is Kinesiology is nothing more than a euphemism for "Advanced Gym Teacher" or "Overly-Educated Masseuse." Understand, most Kinesiology programs are nothing more than a "Sports

Physical Therapy" program (and are sometimes advertised as such) that are designed to attract intellectually lazy students who think it would be "cool" to be the masseuse for professional athletes. If you look at your local university and if they have a Kinesiology program chances are it's not located in the building where the other real bio-science majors are located. It's probably located near the athletic department or the stadium. That is not by coincidence.

In short, if you're going to study Kinesiology, you may as well drop your major and pursue a real discipline in the bio-sciences and become a doctor or a pharmacist. Otherwise you can look forward to a life-long career as a gym teacher.

"The Business of American is Business"

Engineering and the bio-sciences are not the only general fields where you can find worthwhile degrees in STEM. Another general area of education is business. Depending on the school or university you're thinking about attending, most of the larger or major universities out there have some kind of business school. At these business schools there are several disciplines you can pursue, some of which are well-paying.

Most notable and perhaps the most worthwhile degree is accounting. Though accountants do not make as much as say petroleum engineers or surgeons, they do make a decent salary. Additionally, the academic rigor required for an accounting degree is significantly less than that of a petroleum engineering degree or a surgeon. Furthermore, you can make significantly more money as you continue in your career as an accountant by obtaining your CPA (Certified Public Accountant) certification. This certification is actually more valuable than an MBA and costs significantly less to obtain.

Another worthwhile business degree is a relatively new major called “MIS” or “Management of Information Systems.” This is where you set up and manage the various computer and communications networks of a firm or an employer. Ensuring computers are secure, the computer network is working efficiently, setting up people's e-mails, you become the indispensable “IT Guy” that everybody needs and rarely sees in an unemployment line.

Also worthwhile is a degree in Statistics or sometimes called “Actuarial Science.” Here, colleges may vary where each of these types of majors are offered. Usually, Statistics is offered through the IT school and is considered a pure math degree, while Actuarial Science is essentially a degree in statistics but is offered through the business school. Regardless of where it is offered, “Actuarial Science” is one of those often unheard of degrees because it is not terribly glamorous. An “actuary” is basically a statistician that calculates statistics primarily for the insurance or financial services industries so they can assess risk and set prices for insurance or other financial investments. This doesn't sound exciting, and it isn't, but it's well-paying. The reason why is precisely because it is VERY BORING work. The joke often thrown about in actuarial programs is:

"What do you call an accountant without a personality?"

"An actuary."

And they actually laugh at that joke.

Closely related to Statistics and Actuarial Science is a field called "Econometrics." This is not to be confused with Economics, though it is a sub-study of it. Econometrics is essentially the application of mathematics and statistics to economics. They are also employed by the insurance and financial service industries and like actuaries, econometricians calculate statistics and program "financial models" that are used to predict and forecast business trends, economic growth, "credit scores," etc. Because of the highly-advanced mathematics involved, econometricians have started to morph more and more into computer programmers as the models have become so complex it requires significant computing power to run these models. It is here you'll see some considerable overlap between people with a double major in economics and computer programming.

Statistics, Actuarial Science, Accounting, and Econometrics. You're naturally starting to think that "Finance" might be an equally worthwhile business degree. Your thinking is wrong.

Though most business schools offer a degree in Finance, understand Finance is a worthless degree not because of what you're studying, but because of the field you would be entering. Finance itself is a very practical and helpful skill. It is a combination of accounting, economics and statistics. You essentially become a Jack of All Trades and are able to read financial statements, understand them, model them and make forecasts. However, in becoming a Jack of All Trades, you are a master of none.

Businesses who want accountants, want accountants, not finance majors.

Businesses who want actuaries, want actuaries, not finance majors.

And employers who want econometricians, want econometricians, not finance majors.

But the biggest drawback of a finance degree, and thus why it is worthless, is the industry most likely to employ you is the most corrupt and inept industry in the world:

Banking.

You may be familiar with that little "Housing Bubble" thing that happened in 2008? And that little "Financial Crisis" thing that followed it? Perhaps you even remember that "Dotcom Bubble" thing back in 1999. All disproportionately caused by bankers.

The reason why is bankers are, in general people, who were too lazy to go into engineering, let alone accounting, but still wanted to make a ton of money. But, since they have no tangible skills and were too intellectually lazy to go and develop some, they rely on corruption, nepotism, cronyism, connections and "networking" to make their money. Worse still, they really have no morality about them. They will gladly lend money to somebody who can't afford it, build homes during a housing bubble, or destroy the entire US economy as long as there's a commission check in it for them. And since they wouldn't major in engineering or accounting, what do you suppose they majored in?

Finance.

When you major in Finance, you must understand you are majoring in something barely more moral or ethical than being a lawyer. Not only that, all your peers, bosses and co-workers will also be equally amoral. This ultimately results in an industry where you get ahead not by how much you know, how hard you work, or how much ass you kick, but by who you know, how much you golf, and how much ass you kiss.

How can I make these wild accusations? How can I make these blanketing general statements?

Because I've been a banker for 14 years, I majored in Finance and I regret it every day.

Learn from my mistakes, live a happy, stress-free life and don't bother majoring in Finance.

Plumber > Professor of Underwater Basket Weaving

I was 22 at the time. I had graduated #4 out of my entire class at the University of Minnesota's "esteemed" Carlson School of Management. I graduated six months early, worked full time, put myself through college with no debt, had three internships under my belt and was working as a....

security guard.

I was very depressed and very sad as I felt I had wasted not only three and a half years of my youth, but had put so much effort into it I could have just as well partied more, drank more, chased more girls and ended up in the exact same situation. So, there I sat at my security guard job in some empty downtown building in Minneapolis at 3AM, listening to the Victor Borge CD I had just burned myself that afternoon in the hopes of cheering myself up.

I distinctly remember saying to myself,

"Well, might as well see if I can make some extra money teaching some dance classes at the local community education programs,"

But, being ashamed of it because it had come to "teaching a community ed class" to make ends meet. Plus, I viewed ballroom dancing as purely a social pursuit and actually mocked those who did it as a career.

Fortunately for me at the time there was a fax machine as well as internet access where I was stationed. And since I was working the dog shift, I had all the time in the world to put together a proposal for a swing dance class, print it off, and fax it to the various community education programs.

A week went by.

Two weeks.

Then three.

I figured it was just another effort wasted. Even community education wouldn't hire me. But then two months later I received a call. Then another. Then a third. In one week I scheduled three months of dance classes across the Twin Cities metro.

I showed up at my first class in Eagan, Minnesota. I had brought my stereo-system from my home, burned some CD's with some swing music on it, and arrived early to set up shop. Nobody was there at the moment, but by the time class was to start I had over 50 people in my class. Since I was paid a percentage per person and each person was paying about $40 for the class, I did my calculations and soon realized I was making $350 per hour.

Suddenly I wasn't depressed anymore.

Now, the reason I tell you this story is assuming you're the average high school or college-aged youth you have been bombarded with the importance of going to college. You "must" get a degree. You "must" go to college. You "must" have that college experience or your life is over and you will be flipping burgers as you collect a welfare paycheck and bring up 12 illegitimate children in government subsidized housing.

Or so your elders have told you.

But remember, most people, youth and adults, are incredibly ignorant when it comes to economics. The whole reason for you go to college is because in the past going to college was the ticket to getting a high paying job. Now they tell you to go to college because "that's what you're supposed to do." However, this has had two unintended consequences.

One, the irony in telling EVERYBODY to go to college is that EVERYBODY now has a degree, making today's bachelor's degree the equivalent of the 1950's high school diploma. You have a bachelor's degree? Well yip-yip-yip-yip-yahoo. Everybody does! The labor market is flooded with them, consequently making them worth less.

Two, in the blinding push for youth to go to college, our elders failed to distinguish the forest from the trees. The whole point of going to college was to make it so you could find more steady, more reliable and higher paying employment, not just going for the sake of going. And in this blind rush to force all kids to go to college they overlooked a very great opportunity that existed the entire time for the youth:

Trade school.

Understand a "trade" or a "skill" is ultimately what an employer wants and what's going to make you money. They don't want you to be "well-rounded." They don't want you to have "a diverse background." They don't care if you were the president of the "Yeah For Us Super Happy Fun Time Club" at school. And frankly, they don't care if you went to college to get that degree.

They want you to perform a task or a job that requires a skill or a talent to make them a profit.

Now some “trades” or “skills” obviously require schooling. A brain surgeon has to go to school for 10 years. An astronaut must learn an inordinate amount of engineering and physics, not to mention an amazing set of flying skills. An accountant must learn how to balance the books and do double-entry accounting. But not all valued trades or skills require a four or eight year degree. Matter of fact, some very high-paying trades only require a two year degree and certification.

This makes the trades a GREAT option for those of you who just plain don't want to go to college or just have the common sense to demand you get a bang for your educational buck. It's half the time, it's half the cost, and in nearly all instances they pay more than your average liberal arts degree. Plus, it isn’t like you can’t go back to college to get your bachelors or masters. Of course, not all trades result in you getting paid $350 an hour to do the Rumba. But there are some traditional trades that have always been in demand that pay very good wages.

Electricians are a perfect example. They have a precise skill that is in wide demand whether there’s a recession on or not. Their skill set commands an average salary of $51,000 per year. Plumbers are another perfect example. You may not think them glorious, and the stereotypical “butt crack” comes to mind, but they make

$50,000 a year on average. ASE certified auto mechanics make a commendable $40,000 a year. Chimney sweepers bill out anywhere from $25-$75 an hour. And, if you are into computers, there is a whole assortment of certifications and two year programs. Average salaries range anywhere from $38,000 a year on the low end to upwards of $80,000 on the high end.

However, there is something more fundamental and over-arching about the trades. A vital and important lesson to take from them that just further proves the economic realities of the labor market. Understand, it doesn't matter if you choose to go to the local two year college and get an Associate's in Computer Networking, or if you choose to go on and become the world's next brain surgeon. In both cases you are doing the exact same thing – you're learning an employable skill.

In other words, it doesn't matter how much schooling you have, in the end everybody has to learn a trade because it is trades and skills that land you jobs, not merely just an "education." Ergo, the lowly certified auto mechanic has more in common with a brain surgeon than does a doctoral candidate in sociology because the auto mechanic, like the surgeon, has a skill. The lowly plumber has more in common with the bio-engineer than does a doctorate in philosophy because the plumber, like the bio-engineer, produces something of value. It is because of this, trade schools should not be shunned, but should be considered as a viable option when it comes to your education and a superior option to the humanities or liberal arts.

CHAPTER 4
WHAT **NOT** TO STUDY

In studying what degrees are worthwhile and the economics behind them we should have a pretty good idea of what degrees are worthless and are to be avoided. However, just like "Biology" or "Environmental Engineering," it's not always obvious when a major is worthless. Additionally, an even bigger problem facing youth is that the temptation to pursue an easy worthless degree usually overrides their ability to think clearly, objectively and for the long term. Even though deep down inside they may know they're making a mistake, they often ignore those concerning whispers and pursue a worthless degree anyway, or worse, get talked into attending a "degree mill." Four years later they're unemployed, living at home with mom and are now saddled with $50,000 in debt. All because they were short sighted and couldn't resist the false promises of a worthless degree. It is therefore very important to highlight and identify these worthless degrees and re-emphasize that they are indeed (to quote Ed Rooney)...

"a first class ticket to nowhere."

"Thank You, Captain Obvious"

School sucks. And if you were like me, you mastered the art of feigning a fever by putting your head near a heat vent before going up to your mother and telling her to feel your forehead so you could get out of school. So there you sit at home, having the benefit of sleeping in and watching morning cartoons, but by 10AM or 11AM the worst creation in America takes over – daytime TV. You are now no longer regaled by Bugs Bunny or Johnny Bravo, but have to suffer through Oprah, Judge Judy, Jerry Springer and a myriad of soap operas. But if the shows weren't bad enough, the commercials were maddening. And so there you sit, your brain slowly melting and your IQ going down the toilet.

However, there is something notable that should be pointed out about the commercials. In addition to advertisements for bathroom cleaners or various kitchen aids, without fail there are always commercials for some fly-by-night school you never heard of. Some kind of "institute" where *"You too can have an exciting career in 'medical transcriptioning!'"* Or *"Live your dream and become a chef!"* Or *"Enjoy a rewarding career in radio broadcasting!"* And none of these commercials would be complete without mentioning *"You can earn your degree in just 16 short months!"*

Wow! Sounds too good to be true! And you're right, it is too good to be true. The reason is these commercials are advertisements for "degree mills."

Degree mills are nothing more than non-accredited, for-profit institutions that have one goal – to get your money. How do I know this? Because I worked for two of them. They're not there to educate you. They're not there to help you. They're there to get your money. And they prey on youth by exploiting their single biggest weakness – the temptation of a degree with little to no effort in a very short period of time. Not just an easy degree, but a degree that promises you an "exciting career" in a field that sounds so shucks-howdy-gee-whillikers-dandy.

Chefs, radio show hosts, models, singers, artists, unicorn breeders, you name it.

Now most of you (or at least I hope "most of you") are probably rolling your eyes and saying,

"Yes, we know these are scams. You don't have to tell us."

But, much as I would like to say I don't have to write this, millions of naïve youth attend these colleges every year and spend billions of dollars on these worthless programs. Worse still, the average degree mill charges more than your average accredited public university putting their average victim in even more debt. And even worse than that, they aren't accredited. Meaning your credits won't transfer and most employers don't consider it a real college. Therefore, my goal is not just to help prevent these young adults from making the worst mistake of their lives, but to do whatever I can to make sure these "schools" don't get one dime in revenue and go the way of the dinosaur.

Degree mills are actually quite easy to identify. You can assume any "culinary school" or "beauty school" is a degree mill. Talk to any successful chef or any high-end salonist and you'll find most of them never went to school to learn what they did. They just started working as a chef or a hairdresser, had a natural talent for it, and moved up in the field.

Any school offering any kind of program in radio, television, sports broadcasting or film is also a degree mill. Just like the chefs and salonists above, you'll find most radio show personalities never went to "broadcasting school." They literally just fell into broadcasting. Every talk show host or radio show host I've ever known (including myself) never spent a day attending "broadcast journalism school." Matter of fact, we don't even know how we landed the gig in the first place. Of course, all of our support staff spent thousands of dollars on broadcast school, but they were never behind the mic.

Another dead giveaway is the commercials. Not so much that they're on during the daytime and are thusly targeting unemployed losers who might be desperate enough to attend these schools, but they always have these cheesy, lame computer graphics. Commensurate with this is they will always offer a “graphic design” program or a “video game design” program, which behooves the question:

“How crappy is your graphic or computer design program that this commercial is the best you could come up with?”

And finally, the tell-tale sign the school is a degree mill is if they have their school located in a strip mall or an office building. They won't have a “campus.” It won't be located on prime real estate. Degree mills are always housed in ugly, minimalistic, drab 1970's office buildings and strip malls, never in buildings with ornate classical Roman architecture.

Ultimately, if you want to know if the school you are contemplating is a legitimate one you can always consult two lists. The first one is Wikipedia's list of unaccredited institutions:

http://en.wikipedia.org/wiki/List_of_unaccredited_instit utions_of_higher_learning

And the other is the US Department of Education's database on accredited colleges:

http://www.ope.ed.gov/accreditation/

Both lists identify which schools are real ones and which are scams.

Assuming, however, you are smart enough not to attend a degree mill, and you are accepted into a real, accredited college, keep in mind you're not out of the woods yet. Matter of fact, you may be led into a false sense of security. The perfect examples are students who get accepted into top notch schools like Harvard or Yale, but then throw it all away by majoring in a worthless subject. Plus, as you'll find out, there are a lot of professors, teachers assistants, administrators, college deans and other people whose paychecks depend on getting students to spend tuition dollars on their particular programs or departments. In other words, nobody is going to be forthright and honest with you and say,

"Oh, god no! Don't spend your tuition dollars here! You'll never make any money. Go next door to the engineering department. They'll be able to help."

But I will be, and we start with liberal arts programs.

The Liberal Arts and Humanities

The "liberal arts," which are also called "the humanities," are the single biggest concentration of worthless degrees in the accredited world of education. Additionally, they pose the single biggest financial threat to today's young adults and are arguably the single biggest lie perpetrated upon today's college students. Just like their degree mill counterparts, they are worthless. They do absolutely nothing to help you find a job and are not worth the time or the money you spend "earning" them. But what makes them particularly insidious is that they have the legitimacy of being endorsed or ordained by accredited colleges and universities. This gives them a false air of authenticity, making them that much easier of a sell to naive 17 year-olds who don't know any better.

In general, liberal arts can be summarily described as "degrees that avoid math at all costs." This, once again, makes them an easier sell to young adults looking for an easy major, but it also makes them worthless because as we learned in chapter two, math is the key for a successful career in the future. They can also be identified by what kind of degree you are awarded should you graduate. In general, worthless degrees are denoted with a "B.A." or "Bachelor of Arts," while worthwhile degrees are denoted with a "B.S." or

"Bachelor of Science." These general rules aside, it is important to look at each type of liberal arts degree individually and realize why they are worthless and why you should avoid them.

"Hyphenated-American Studies"

You won't see "Hyphenated American Studies" listed in any college course book. But you will see "African-American Studies," "Chicano-American Studies," "Asian-American Studies," "Gay/Bi/Lesbian/Transgender-American Studies," "Women's Studies," etc., etc. Frankly, these are particularly dirty and low degrees in that not only are they worthless, but they target minority groups as their victims. Even "dirtier and lower" than that, is they presumably purport themselves to be degrees that would help these various groups of people, when in reality all they do is impoverish minority groups that already have an uphill battle.

The problem with these degrees is that they tug at the heart strings of people by identifying with their gender, culture, race, sexuality, etc., etc. However, when all is said and done, these degrees do nothing to genuinely help these individuals. For example my buddy Richard, who is black, likes to play video games. My buddy Khan, who is gay, likes racing cars. No matter how much Richard studies "being black" or Khan "being gay" it won't help either of them purchase a gaming console or a souped-up car. The reason is these degrees study traits, they don't study or develop skills. You can't study to become "really Asian" just as you can't study to become "really gay." You either are gay or Asian or you're not. There is no employable skill in merely having a trait you were born with. But you can study to become a really great engineer. Or a really great accountant. Or a really great surgeon. Because those things are skills.

Now, this isn't to say that studying or reading about African American history or the history of gays in America isn't interesting. Nor is it to say you shouldn't maybe pick up a book and read about it. But that's the point right there. Why spend $5,000 a quarter on tuition to pay some old, bitter washed-up professor who got suckered into this "profession" 20 years ago to tell you about "Women's Studies" when you can simply pick up a book at the library and read it for free? You'll get the exact same benefit and education with the exact same employment prospects, but without the $80,000 tuition bill.

"Foreign Culture Studies"

Akin to the "hyphenated-American studies" are "foreign culture studies." Here you're not studying about African Americans or Middle-Eastern Americans. You're studying about Africa and the Middle East. In other words, it's the exact same degree, just not domestic. You're studying the actual cultures of foreign places.

The criticisms of these degrees are nearly identical to that of the "hyphenated-American" degrees. Since there's no upshot in terms of your employability, why not just get books at the library for free and read up on these places and cultures? But there's an even bigger flaw in these degrees that really shows you just how worthless they are. If you're studying foreign countries and foreign cultures, why not just go there? Why pay some washed up professor $4,500 a quarter in tuition to tell you about China, when you can (oh, I don't know) TAKE THE $4,500 AND ACTUALLY VISIT CHINA???

"Foreign Languages"

Continuing on our foreign theme is foreign languages. Foreign languages are not completely worthless in that the world does need translators. But you'd be surprised how little translators actually make. Around $39,000 per year according to the US Department of Labor, and that's mid-career, not starting salary.

However, there is a more important reason to avoid majoring in a foreign language:

The job you'll most likely end up with.

Realize there is a 99.9% chance you'll end up teaching middle school, high school or college age kids a foreign language they don't want to learn, they'll never use, and will forget within six months. You know how you took those two years of Spanish back in the 8th and 9th grades? Yeah, how's that Spanish coming along now? I took two years of college German and I learned more German playing "Call of Duty" and "Medal of Honor."

"Rennt um eure leben, er hat 'en panzerfaust!"

Yeah, that right there cost me $1,200 in tuition back in the 1990's. A degree in a foreign language will certainly cost you more.

"Art/Music/Theater/Dance/Film/Art History"

This one should be pretty self-explanatory, but I'm going to explain it anyway. Understand degrees in the arts are not just worthless, but pointless on many levels. First is the "professional athlete" paradox.

Just like professional athletes, you stand an equally dismal chance of becoming a famous actor or singer or dancer. One in 14,000. You can get your doctorate in poetry or dance or what have you, but unless you've got the rare talent of Michelangelo or Duke Ellington, no amount of schooling will help you.

Second, take a look at Michelangelo or Duke Ellington, or for that matter the majority of successful artists, musicians, actors and singers. You'll notice something they have in common. Not one of them have their masters or doctorate in the fields they excelled in. Even

I am an accomplished ballroom dancer, and I never took one ballroom dancing class in college. How is it that myself, Mike, and The Duke all mastered one form of an art or another? The answer is practice. Not schooling.

Understand the arts are simply that, arts. They cannot be taught, they can only be achieved through practice, passion and a desire to become a good musician, actor or dancer. Yes, it helps to study under someone to master the basics, but if you wish to excel in it and become a truly unique "artist," that is something only you can do through your unique vision and skill. In short, studying what other people have done is mere mimicry. This is why Jimmy Hendrix is a true artist and anyone with an advanced degree in the performing arts are mere wannabe's. Be a true artist, don't be a wannabe. Practice your passion, but don't pay somebody to tell you how to do it.

"English"

English has got to be the most worthless degree in the entire English-speaking world. The reason why should be blindingly obvious. YOU ALREADY SPEAK ENGLISH! If you are 18 years old and got accepted into an accredited college, then it's a pretty safe bet you're fluent enough in English. You can read it, write it and speak it pretty darn well by now. The only possible reason I can see people choosing English as a major is if they wish to speak it "real good."

The solution to this should be very apparent. If you are not comfortable with your reading, writing or speaking skills in your native language, then simply practice it more. Don't spend an inordinate amount of time and money paying somebody else to teach it to you. Or, to quote my 7th grade self when my English teacher was lecturing me about not handing in my assignment on time:

"Yeah, must have taken a lot to major in a subject that not only were you fluent in, but so were all of your future students."

I do believe I was summarily sent to the principal's office.

"Creative Writing"

Along the same lines of English is "Creative Writing." This is a new one that arose in response to, frankly, mid-life-crisis women wanting to become the next JK Rowling. But instead of just writing a book (which would be too easy), they thought they first needed to get a degree in creative writing.

Notice again, we see some recurring traits that were apparent in other worthless degrees. Take, for instance, the "creative" or artistic aspect of this degree. How do you teach somebody to be creative? You can't. But you sure can charge them $3,750 a semester in tuition to act like you are. And akin to English, if you're not comfortable with your writing skills, what do you think is the better option? Practice? Or paying somebody $3,750 a semester to tell you to practice?

The honest truth with creative writing, or any writing for that matter, is you don't need any post-secondary schooling for it. Just go and write. If you look at the world's most famous authors very few of them had their "Masters Degree in English." They simply had a passion for it and they just started writing books. Heck, even I flunked out of 7th grade English (for obvious reasons) and still managed to write two books. Meanwhile, ironically, most people who have degrees in English or "Creative Writing" are either never published or, if they are, nobody has ever heard of their works.

"Literature"

You are paying somebody to tell you to read.

"Communications/Linguistics/Rhetoric"

I couldn't believe it when I saw it, but when I was researching what the congressmen and women at the Minnesota State Legislature had studied in college, I saw somebody with a degree in "Rhetoric." At the time, I didn't believe it was a real degree. How do you study something as simple as rhetoric for four years? But, sure enough, it's a real major and offered by many colleges. Some universities even have a Department of Rhetoric.

Rhetoric falls under a general category of equally worthless majors titled "Communications" or "Linguistics." The purpose of these majors is to make it so you understand a language in great detail and can therefore use it to communicate clearly to other people. Without a degree in communications it's impossible to communicate clearly. For example, right now you have no idea what I'm talking about, nor what the past several chapters of this book were about because neither you nor I have degrees in communications. You also are clearly incapable of communicating with your friends over e-mail or texting because none of you have degrees in communications. And when you sit at the dinner table with your parents, you see their mouths move, you hear something, but it's just noise. Matter of fact, it's amazing anything gets done at all in this world given that communications majors account for such a small percent of the population.

"Anthropology"

Like Communications, I had to look up "Anthropology" to find out precisely what it was. I had heard of Anthropology majors before, but the few I met I wasn't terribly impressed with. They weren't particularly interesting, they weren't particularly smart, and one of them was just outright mean. Turns out that wasn't a coincidence.

Anthropology is the study of (are you ready for it?)

"Humanity."

What makes it worse is I've just spent 15 minutes researching "anthropology" on the internet and I still can't figure out what its point or purpose is. But, I do actually know something about Anthropology. You can expect to spend a lot of time in the unemployment line if you major in it while your student debt accrues interest.

"Political Science/Public Administration"

Political science has got to be the laziest major for the most dangerous people. The reason why is not only is it an easy major, thus attracting the lazier elements of society, it is a tell-tale sign somebody has political aspirations.

Now, political aspirations are one thing if you served in the military for 30 years, or ran a successful business for 30 years, or you're considering retirement but would like to participate in democracy and give back to the community by sharing some of your wisdom. But when you are 17 and decide to major in "Political Science" you are essentially admitting two things. One, you are a power hungry child who should never hold public office.

Two, you are too lazy to do any real work (thereby earning the right to be a leader of men) because you think real work is beneath you. In short, you are one of the most despicable people.

How, at the age of 17, 18 or 19, do you think you have the wisdom or intelligence to run for public office? Additionally, what real world, hardening experiences do you have at such a young age that you dare to think you should be in a position of leadership? And, what qualifications do you have over older, wiser, more-experienced and less lazy people?

Public office is not a career, or at least it shouldn't be. And, depending on how much you pay attention to politics, you'll note career politicians and a lack of term limits are two of the main reasons we have the problems we do today in society.

So, instead of becoming part of the problem, why don't you do something useful like flip burgers or dig a ditch? Matter of fact, with the arrogant attitude it takes to major in Political Science, why don't you just stay out of society altogether?

"Philosophy"

Philosophy is, again, one of those majors that may be very interesting, but you can achieve the exact same thing by reading books for free at the library and have the exact same employment prospects. I remember teaching part-time at the Perpich School of the Arts in Minnesota. Naturally, the majority of students were going to major in something worthless. But when I heard this kid say, "Well I'm going to major in Philosophy," even his fellow students were ripping him apart. Not because they wanted to belittle him, but because even they knew the major was worthless and cared enough about their friend to cajole him out of it. Again, if you want to read Plato and Socrates, read Plato and Socrates. Do not take the unnecessary step of paying some pony-tail-wearing 1960's hippie $3,900 to do so.

"Psychology"

To be blunt, Psychology, specifically "Child Psychology" is what girls who don't like math major in. When I was in high school, pretty much every girl there wanted to become a "child psychologist." Of course, at the time they were no more than children themselves and certainly did not have the life experience or wisdom to be dishing out psychological advice to anyone. Matter of fact, most of them had pretty deep psychological problems themselves and would make the world's worst therapists. But that thought never really occurs to people pursuing degrees in Psychology, because deep down inside they don't really care about their clients, they just care about themselves. They just want an easy degree.

Hypocrisy aside, there is another major drawback to majoring in Psychology. That drawback is the degree is completely worthless unless you move on to get your masters or doctorate in the field. A Masters in Psychology will allow you to consult people under the tutelage of a clinic or institution, however the pay will not be great. It is only once you get your doctorate that you can go into practice for yourself and make a decent living. So, if you are going to pursue a degree in Psychology lock yourself in and commit yourself to getting a doctorate. Otherwise, it is a waste of your time.

"Journalism"

Journalism has that wonderful combination of arrogance that Political Science majors have, with the added bonus of being in an industry that has completely collapsed. Usually, Journalism majors are young, inexperienced kids that once again arrogantly think the rest of us care to hear what they have to say. Making matters worse, most Journalism majors are on some kind of political vendetta or crusade thinking they're going to "change the world," when in reality, good journalists merely report the truth and have no agenda.

But, the primary reason you'll want to be avoiding Journalism as a profession is that the industry is dead. It's based on newspapers. Newspapers that have since been replaced with the internet, full of bloggers who now do the jobs of journalists for free. And good luck finding a job at one of the few remaining publications that are still in business. Their ranks are filled with Baby Boomer and Gen X journalists desperately clinging onto their jobs. Do you think they're going to forfeit their positions just to let you get a job?

Do yourself a favor. Instead of majoring in Journalism, start a blog. It's a lot cheaper.

"Frankenstein Degrees"

In the never-ending effort to extract more tuition dollars from more people, colleges and universities started offering "interdisciplinary" degrees. These degrees allow a person to tailor or create their own degree from whatever subjects or majors they wish. The problem with interdisciplinary degrees is that if there was enough demand in the market for a degree that needed to be a combination of two or more fields, universities and colleges were usually pretty good at rolling it out as an official degree. Petroleum engineering is an example where the demands to combine chemistry and engineering in the labor market resulted in a legitimate program being offered at the university. Econometrics is another example where demands of the insurance industry required a combination of economics and computer programming.

Unfortunately, this means if you have to resort to creating your own degree, chances are it's not in demand. And if you look at the majority of interdisciplinary degrees, they're pretty worthless. I remember one friend of mine combining Kinesiology with Business Management because she wanted to run her own Kinesiology practice where "all of the professional athletes would come to visit when they needed therapy" (ignoring the fact all professional sports teams already have masseuses on staff). Another, if I recall correctly, was where Women's Studies was combined with Architecture to create "feminist buildings." Understand, what makes these degrees worthless is putting what the student wants ahead of what is in demand in the market. If it worked the other way, heck, I would have gladly gotten a "Masters in Jennifer Aniston, Rumpleminze, F-18, Call of Duty, Motorcycle, X-Box 360 Studies." In the meantime, do not bother with the "Frankenstein" degrees.

"New Age Crap"

As you may have surmised, you cannot get a "Bachelors of Art in New Age Crap." However, this is a catch-all category to account for the many and varied majors that have come out in the past decade solely to capitalize on people's willingness to spend their tuition dollars on hobbies and not real degrees.

The Masters in Puppetry is the perfect example of a

degree that is nothing more than a hobby. It's quite obvious any student of this discipline is not a serious one and deep down inside hopes somebody else in society is going to take care of them. "Holistic Medicine" is another faux degree designed to capitalize on the mid-life crisis market as well as the "green fad." And "Music Therapy" is for those musicians who aren't that good and want to be lied to about the usefulness of their skills (you'd be amazed how many Music Therapy majors there are).

There is, however, a whole sub-segment of "New Age Crap" degrees that theme around politics and these are the ones you have to look out for. The reason being, much like our "Environmental Engineering" degree was the result of political propaganda predisposing youth into worthless fields, these degrees do the same.

A perfect example is "Environmental Studies." At least with Environmental Engineering, there is some engineering involved. But its much watered-down cousin, Environmental Studies is completely worthless. Unfortunately, too many youth drank the environmentalist purple-punch in school and still chose to major in it anyway.

"Peace Studies" is another popular "fad" degree and really didn't exist until the invasion of Iraq. This degree is designed to take advantage of young pacifists, portraying the concept of pacifism as an actual discipline that can be studied and, worse, turned into a career. In reality, peace is a status between nations, not an industry that is hiring right now.

Also closely related to "Peace Studies" is "Social Justice." If you're going to major in "Social Justice" be honest about it. You really don't want to work. You don't like the fact you have to grow up and support yourself. So, you're going to join the other equally intellectually dishonest adult-children and whine and complain about how "unjust" this society is, finding ways, if not creating them out of whole cloth to rationalize taking other people's money. All so you can avoid a real job, while still make-believing you're an adult because you have a degree. Don't worry, you're not fooling anyone.

"Education"

Unlike in years past, a degree in Education today is effectively a degree in "Baby Sitting." It is the degree selfish, lazy people major in because they know you get three months a year off for vacation and they think being a teacher is an easy job. They are arguably even more arrogant than Political Science majors because they are choosing the degree not for the kids they intend to educate, but first and foremost for themselves. They are simply using the kids. This is not to say all teachers majored in education for themselves and didn't put the kids first. This is to say the majority of them did.

Most people will disagree with this, but honestly ask yourself how many teachers really did a good job in your K-12 education? And, if you're in college, how many professors or teachers assistants are just stellar by your standards? How many of them made their subject interesting? How many of them took the time to convey the concepts clearly so you could understand them? Or, was it the case where they were they all too lazy to put the effort into keeping you intellectually engaged during school? They were so mind-numbingly boring you had to fight just to stay awake in class? That they were just coming to a job to collect a paycheck and couldn't give a damn less about their students? I bet if you did the math you could count all the really good teachers on one hand.

Furthermore, just look at any of your peers who are declaring Education majors. Sure, one or two of them might have expressed a genuine interest in educating children in the past, but for the most part if you ask your fellow students why they're majoring in Education, "three months a year vacation" will inevitably be listed as one of the primary reasons. This belies the true quality and caliber of Education majors.

There is, however, some merit in majoring in Education which makes Education one of the few liberal art degrees with a couple saving graces. First, there is a market for teachers. Billions of dollars a year are spent on hiring teachers so there are jobs out there. Second, being a teacher is very important. Educating children so they develop the skills and abilities to have successful futures is not just noble, but vital for society.

The question is whether you are majoring in Education for the right reasons. If you're just going into Education because deep down inside you know babysitting a bunch of rug-rats is going to require less work and rigor than becoming an accountant, then you are, frankly, a despicable person. But, if you really do care about the kids, and you really do care about the future of the country, choosing to become a teacher is not just altruistic, but very noble.

Worthless Business Degrees

When you think of a business degree, you usually think "practical" or "useful." A degree in one of the business disciplines would obviously be designed to be used in business and therefore would be a very employable major. However, while some business degrees are worthwhile like Accounting, a surprising number of them are actually quite worthless.

"Business"

It may sound too simple, but you can get a degree in just plain ol' "Business." Sometimes they call it "Business Administration" but whatever the name, the degree is worthless. The reason is two-fold.

First "business" is not a specific skill or a trade. You don't practice business like you would accounting or computer networking. It's something you do and get experience in over time. Most "businessmen" didn't get their MBA or business degree, they just went into business because they had an idea and learned it as they went along. So when you approach an employer with a "Business" degree you're basically saying,

"I have no experience and no skills, but I read about a lot of businessmen at school."

Second, the concept of Business Administration suggests that at the young age of 22 you're going to manage a business. Oh really? Fresh out of college, not an ounce of experience and you're going to be put in charge of an entire division or a region? Heck, why not put you in charge of the whole company? One thing I did notice while attending business school was how many classes and seminars were offered on "leadership." And I always found it hypocritical because precisely how do you teach "leadership?" Was there a formula? Is there a how-to manual? And, if there is a manual or a formula, then everybody should be leaders! It's the ultimate in hypocrisy because it presumes reading about leadership and studying it trumps actual experience and skills.

What it ultimately boils down to is that employers are not looking to give any rookie 22 year old any kind of managerial, administrative or leadership position. Unfortunately, that's all a Business Administration degree is. So, don't waste your time getting a degree in bland, beige "Business." Get a degree that gives you a skill such as Accounting, MIS or Actuarial Science. It will not only help you find employment, it will get you to a leadership position faster than any "leadership seminar or retreat."

"Entrepreneurship"

Getting a degree in Entrepreneurship is an oxymoron. The whole point and purpose of becoming an entrepreneur is because you want to work for yourself. But the whole point of earning a degree is to get a job working for somebody else. So why would you get a degree in Entrepreneurship? And how would that work when applying for a job of a different employer?

"Why did you major in Entrepreneurship?"

"Because I wanted to work for myself."

"Then why are you here?"

I always laughed at Entrepreneurship majors because the mere action of majoring in it showed you they simply did not have the personality and aggression to become a real entrepreneur. And, as it just so happens, most Entrepreneurship degrees teach you more or less the exact same thing a Business Administration degree would – nothing.

If you are an entrepreneur or you want to become one, going to college is simply a waste of valuable money and time that could be spent on starting your business. And while you may want to major in Entrepreneurship to pick up those accounting, legal or financial skills that are vital to managing your business, realize you can pick up those skills on the cheap by either reading books about them, taking your local community education course or ideally going to Khan's Academy ™ to learn about it for free.

Don't be the laughing stock of the business school, be an entrepreneur that employs the graduates of the business school.

"Marketing/Advertising"

Marketing or "Advertising" can be summed up in one simple sentence:

"The more you spend on advertising the higher your sales will be."

I don't care how many college courses they offer in it, I don't care if you can actually earn a doctorate in the field. All the books and all the lectures in the entire world of marketing can be succinctly summarized as:

"The more you spend on advertising the higher your sales will be."

The problem with degrees like this is not that they are worthless. Nor is the problem with degrees like this is that your only form of employment will be a telemarketer. The problem with these degrees is the psychological torture you must endure trying to stretch out that one sentence into a four, six or eight year degree. Save your brain cells and sanity, and avoid these worthless majors.

"HR/Human Resources/Industrial Relations"

In the olden days, "Human Resources," sometimes called "Industrial Relations," could have been summed up in one simple sentence:

"The more you spend on salaries the higher your employee loyalty will be."

However, HR has gone through a transition for the good, which kind of puts it in the "gray area" as to whether or not it is a worthwhile degree.

The blunt truth is HR was primarily used as an affirmative action program by corporations to get more women into the work force, but they were pigeonholed into the "personnel department" where they could "do the least about of damage." However, two unforeseen developments in the industry changed the HR profession.

One, though "pigeonholed" in the personnel department where they could do "the least amount of damage," HR majors still managed to wreak an incredible amount of damage on companies by impairing their recruiting efforts. The primary culprit was the stereotypical "HR Generalist," a 24 year old naïve woman who, fresh out of college, was on a power trip to screen out candidates willy-nilly. These young women were the first line of defense for recruiting and screening efforts, but because they had no real skills, talent or experience, they were incapable of determining whether job applicants were really qualified or not (imagine an HR generalist with no engineering background trying to intelligently assess the skills of electrical engineers). It took about 15 years, but inevitably, employers started phasing out the "HR Generalists" and requiring the actual bosses to do their own interviewing and recruiting.

The second development was retirement programs. While employers started removing HR from the recruiting process, they moved them to an area called "benefits and compensation." Here HR actually does do some good work. They study salaries and the labor market, create compensation packages, manage retirement programs and insurance programs, as well as ensure companies abide by employment law. It is here, if you want to major in HR, that you should focus your efforts.

However, you can't just major in "HR" and hope to land a job in this stable field of employment. You need to familiarize yourself with things like retirement plans, employment law, benefits and compensation, etc. Therefore, a major in Human Resources combined with a minor in something like Accounting, Finance, or even a seminar on employment law would go a long way in helping you find employment in this field.

"Economics"

Economics will sometimes be offered through a university's business school or sometimes through its liberal arts department. Wherever it is located, it's pretty worthless.

Economics, like psychology, isn't worth anything unless you get an advanced degree. Even if you get an advanced degree, you'll probably end up teaching or working for the government at some bureau doing unglamorous work.

Additionally, Economics suffers from the traits many other worthless degrees have. There's too many people majoring in it, thereby flooding the market and driving its value down. It's a lot like Finance where your primary employer will be banking or the government, both of which are notoriously corrupt. Also like Finance, unless you have a connection or a contact, nobody will hire you. And unless you combine it with something practical like statistics (Econometrics) or computer programming, it's too bland a degree to have any specific or precise skills. Additionally, it's one of those fields where if you want to learn about it, you can simply pick up a book or watch cable news. So no matter how logical it may sound that economics would be a good practical degree, the reality is it's a degree to avoid.

CHAPTER 5
GRAD SCHOOL BLUES AND LITMUS TESTS

So you graduate with a worthless degree, you can't find a job, so what seems like a logical next step?

Grad school! Naturally, of course!

You've been told since you were young that the only thing better than going to college would be going to more college and getting a masters or a doctorate. But, there are some inherent problems in pursuing an advanced degree, not the least of all that it's infinitely more expensive than an undergraduate degree. So, before you decide you're going to double down and commit for another two or four years, you might want to take another look at advanced degrees before you take the big plunge.

"MBA's/Masters in Business Administration"

MBA's perfectly highlight the single biggest risk of pursuing an advanced degree – a flooded market. Understand, with the 2008 financial crisis and the recession that ensued, the United States went through its longest period of high unemployment since the Great Depression. The unemployment rate has been above 9% for the past 2 ½ years and at the time this book was written, still remains above 9%. Because of such a long period of unemployment, people naturally started looking at going back to school to increase their skills so that when the economy "came roaring back" they'd be posed with even better skills and credentials.

There's just one problem.

Everybody had the exact same idea.

So, when you look at GMAT test takers (a proxy that shows you how many people are pursuing their MBA's) you see a glut of MBA's are about to hit the market. This flood of MBA's makes the value of the degree go down.

OF GMAT TEST TAKERS (Source:GMAC)

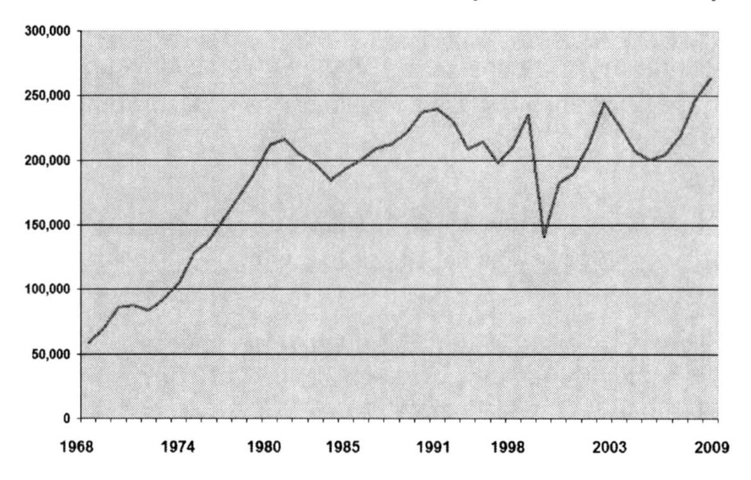

The problems of the MBA do not stop here. There is also the matter of the reputation of the MBA. Back in the 1960's and 1970's when MBA's were rare, sure, they had a good reputation and why not? Back then, very few people pursued advanced degrees. But as more and more schools started offering MBA programs and more and more people started to avail themselves of the opportunity, the quality and caliber of the average MBA went down. And it wasn't without consequences. If you look at every major economic crisis we've had, you will see MBA's were right there at the top of it, if not pushing it along.

The Dotcom Bubble - Full of MBA's idiotically financing worthless dotcom businesses that had no chance of ever making money.

The Accounting Scandals (Enron and Andersen Accounting) – Again, chock full of MBA's heading up these firms and squarely to blame for the accounting scandal.

The Housing Bubble/Great Recession – Surprise, surprise, MBA's were at the helm again.

In short, MBA's are not the financial gurus that everybody thinks they are. Matter of fact, they're starting to get the reputation of being overpaid, incompetent, "yes-men" that just follow trends and pilot their companies into bankruptcy.

The MBA's reputation is also not helped by the increasing number of "fad" MBA's suggesting the degree has "jumped the shark." You can now get an MBA in "Corporate Social Responsibility." Or an MBA in "Sustainability." Even if there isn't a specialization that comes with the title, all one has to do is go to the local business school, look up the course requirements of the MBA, and you'll see it's the exact same classes as a Bachelors in Business Administration with a 50% more expensive price tag. Some just make you take cute little extra classes to further specialize your degree.

Finally, let's look at the price tag of an MBA. You don't think those deans and administrators at all these business schools dared to increase tuition costs to take advantage of the millions of people now returning to school do you? Depending on the source, it costs roughly a cool $100,000 in tuition to get an MBA, and prices are only going up. This is, of course, offset by financial aid, but can you afford not to have a job after that?

The truth is the MBA is simply an overpriced, over-hyped degree. As time goes on and the market is flooded with more of them, they will become less unique and therefore less valuable. Furthermore, as you'll find out when you get older, unless you have connections or your last name is "Rockefeller," chances are you'll just be indebting yourself to a crippling level. Instead, I highly recommend getting an undergrad in Accounting and then pursuing your CPA. Not only is a CPA much cheaper ($3,000 for all the exam and fees,) you'll have even better earnings potential than the average MBA.

"Law Degrees"

The single largest concentration of worthless degrees is the liberal arts. And the single largest destination for liberal arts majors who can't find jobs is law school.

Law degrees are much like MBA's, just even more depraved of morality and integrity. It is not a coincidence that those too lazy to pursue a real degree end up in law school. Just look at the undergrad degrees most lawyers have and you'll see very few Engineering majors or accountants, but you'll see a ton of Sociology majors and hyphenated-American studies majors. But this disproportionate representation of liberal arts degrees also goes a long way in explaining why lawyers have the bad (and well-deserved) reputation they do.

Starting in elementary school, children are told how great and wonderful they are. You could even say they're brainwashed to think too highly of themselves and certainly are brainwashed today to have an entitlement mentality. These kids continue on through high school and when it comes time to pick a major they never consider the real-world ramifications of picking a worthless degree because the entire time they've been told how wonderful they are and how successful they'll be. Sure enough, a disproportionately high number of them choose the liberal arts. Because it's nearly impossible to get anything below a 3.5 GPA in the liberal arts, their egos and entitlement mentalities are only reinforced. It isn't until they graduate and can't find a job is their fragile little world shattered. However, undaunted, they continue on to law school, work very hard for two years, and after incurring another $75,000 in debt, they still can't find a job (or at least a decent paying one).

By this time, you have a person who has been told they deserve the world for the past 20 years. The world, however, is not complying. But this person has a law degree and huge student debts, not to mention in their minds they think they worked really hard for the past six years. What do you think this person is going to do?

Of course this person is going to do whatever they can to make money whether it's moral or not. Frivolous lawsuits. Chasing ambulances. Concocted class-action lawsuits. They're entitled to it! However, more commonly today, you see lawyers join political crusades. The primary purpose of which is to extract money from either political donors, charities or the taxpayers under some kind of "social justice" theme. A lot will follow the rule, "those who can't do teach" and return to Academia where they will become bitter, angry professors. And a lot of them, if their parents have the money, will simply enter politics (go and see if your representatives in government have law degrees and hail from well-to-do families).

If this isn't enough to make you think twice about becoming a lawyer, there is one more important bit of data that every youth should know before attending law school - starting pay.

It is common knowledge that lawyers make a lot of money, right? Well that's if you went to only the top tier law schools or for those of you with the last name of "Rockefeller." A very dirty underhanded trick law schools like to do is cite the "mean" starting salary of law graduates, but say nothing of the "median" starting salary of law graduates. The reason why is because a handful of lawyers make a ton of money out of school which brings the mean average up. But unless you went to one of those top tier schools and are one of those top tier lawyers you can expect to make (are you ready for it?) a little more than an undergrad in a worthless degree.

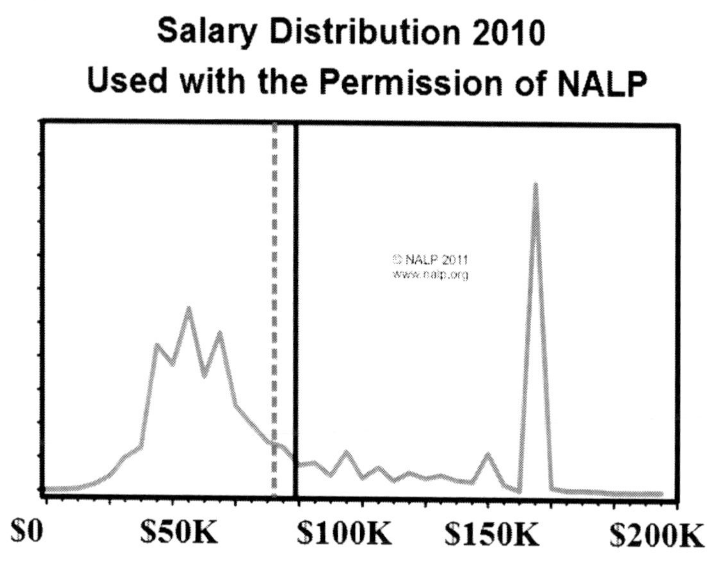

So, if you are currently contemplating law school as the next step in your career, compare the price tag of law school against the first hump in the chart above. Not the "mean average" the law school is telling you.

"Doubling Down"

The final mistake you can make with an advanced degree is doubling down on a worthless one. If you couldn't find a job with a Bachelors of Arts in Philosophy, what makes you think you'll find one with a masters or a doctorate? You already made one mistake that cost you four years of your youth and $40,000 in tuition. Why make the same mistake that will cost you an additional two years and $60,000?

Litmus Tests

There are literally hundreds of degrees and this book just covers some of the main and most popular ones. But, if you're still not sure whether a degree is worthless, there are some quick tests you can apply to see if they're worthless or not.

"The Regurgitation of Classes"

A friend of mine got his "Masters in Educational Leadership" and though originally excited about it at first, he was quickly let down when he realized that all the masters program was, was a regurgitating of the same three classes over and over again.

"Leadership in Education"

"Educational Leadership."

"Leading in Education."

"Fundamentals of Leadership."

For two years, in a presumably "advanced program," he learned nothing new and nothing that he already didn't know from 12 years of teaching.

This is a hallmark of worthless degrees. There is no real substance to the "major" and so they take the one or two themes that do have some value and constantly regurgitate them over and over again (all the while charging you $335 a credit for it, which is the actual price my friend was paying).

Avoid these majors.

"800 Page Book Out of a Sentence"

Related to the regurgitation of classes is when they take a simple concept and stretch it out into an 800 page textbook. I fondly remember having to read about "Porter's Five Forces Model" in business school which said businesses are affected by five different forces. I believe they were internal, external, economy, customer and suppliers. Whatever the case, something as simple and common sense as that should just be stated and you move on.

Oh, no. Not for the Porter's Five Forces Model.

We spent a whole freaking week on that stupid model and I think there was an entire chapter dedicated to that stupid concept in the book.

Now, going through several years of school yourself, you may have already experienced this. You are trying to read a book, but it is just so damn boring your brain can barely stay awake, let alone retain anything. Normally, either your teachers or your parents will assume "you're just not motivated." or "you're a bad student," but a more likely explanation is that there really isn't much to be said about the subject and your brain is just naturally shutting down because it's not learning anything new or practical. But, never let "usefulness" or "practicality" get in the way of an academian trying to make themselves sound important by extrapolating 750 pages from a mere sentence or two.

Whatever the case, you'll see this phenomenon most often in business school where simple concepts are often stretched into full college level classes. Marketing is a perfect example. How do you extract 800 pages, let alone a full doctoral program from the sentence:

"If you spend more money on advertising, your sales will go up."

They manage to do it, but you don't have to suffer through it. Don't major in these subjects.

"Forced to Buy the Textbook"

Speaking of textbooks, when you get to college you'll have to buy a lot of them. And surprise, surprise, the book you have to buy is the book written by your professor! Not only is it by the same professor, it's pretty expensive too! And I wonder what the chances are that he'll come out with a new edition every year so you can't buy the year-old used book as he'll force you to buy the new one! I'm so happy people in the education industry care about your education and not making money off of you.

Since people with worthless degrees can only offer you worthless products or services, there's really no demand for their products. That is, of course, unless they can force you to buy it either through the public schools or coercive legislation through the government. So when you find yourself being forced to buy something that you really don't need, chances are, if you dig deep enough, you'll find somebody with a worthless degree at the heart of it.

The question is who do you want to be?

The women's studies professor forcing unsuspecting freshman to buy her unreadable 500 page book, "The

Pedagogy of the Patriachy of Male Dominance," for $225?

Or the guy at the video game store spreading video gaming happiness and mirth throughout the world?

That's what I thought.

"DIY"

A very simple test you can run asks the question:

"Can I get the exact same education by either buying a product or doing it myself?"

For example, here are some degrees that cost you roughly $30,000 in tuition, their much cheaper replacements, and the savings you'd realize:

Degree	Replacement	Savings
Foreign Languages	Language Software	$29,721
Philosophy	Read Socrates	$29,980
Women's Studies	Watch Daytime TV	$30,000
Journalism	Start a blog	$30,000
Radio/Broadcasting	Apply	$30,000
Political Science	Listen to talk radio	$30,000
Theater	Audition for a play	$30,000
Literature	Go to the library	$30,000
English	Speak English	$30,000

Since none of these degrees help increase your employability, you might as well just avoid these majors, as well as their hefty price tags, and do it on your own.

"Pablum"

Read the following:

"The social and cultural sub-field has been heavily influenced by structuralists and post-modern theories, as well as a shift toward the analysis of modern societies. During the 1970s and 1990s there was an epistemological shift away from the positivist traditions that had largely informed the discipline. During this shift, enduring questions about the nature and production of knowledge came to occupy a central place in cultural and social anthropology. In contrast, archaeology and biological anthropology remained largely positivist. Due to this difference in epistemology, anthropology as a discipline has lacked cohesion over the last several decades." - Wikipedia

"Designed to introduce teachers to the major issues, concepts, paradigms and teaching strategies in multicultural education. It will provide students with a comprehensive overview of multicultural education, a grasp of its complexity, and understanding what that means for educational practice. Characteristics of a multicultural school and the ways in which knowledge of multicultural education can transform the curriculum to

promote the attitudes and skills students need to become effective citizens will be identified and described as well as ways to help students from diverse groups increase their academic achievement." - St.Mary's Masters in Educational Leadership Program

"The Ph.D. program in Feminist Studies and the graduate minor program in Feminist and Critical Sexuality Studies are designed to help students develop a high level of competence in feminist theories, research methods, interdisciplinarity, and pedagogies. Our program is especially strong on feminist theory and issues related to women's diversity, nationally and globally. To guarantee a high level of interdisciplinary exchange, our program is designed to bring Feminist Studies doctoral students together with graduate minor students who are pursuing a disciplinary specialty in their own home department." - University of Minnesota - Women's Studies Department

Is your head hurting? Mine sure is! I didn't understand one damn word that was said and I've had my IQ tested at 141.

The above is what we call "pablum." Nonsensical gibberish that is nothing more than made up words for a made up degree to make those pursuing it sound intelligent when they're really not. Pablum is 100% correlated with worthless degrees because it is merely masking the fact that the study or discipline offers nothing of tangible value to society. It's nothing but euphemism after euphemism to hide the degree's utter worthlessness and hope the program continues to receive funding.

If you see pablum or words like “paradigm” or “rubric” you have a 100% no-money-back guarantee the degree is worthless.

“The Circle of Why Bother”

The cartoon “Archer” has a great scene in it where the hero (Archer) and his friend are talking to an Anthropology major.

Anthropology major - “Hey, guy, my field's anthropology!”

Friend - “Heh heh, well good luck with the job hunt.”

Anthropology major - “Not that it's any of your business, but I plan to teach!”

Archer - “Heh heh, Anthropology?”

Anthropology major - “Yes!”

Friend - “To...uhhhhh...Anthropology majors?”

Archer - “Ha! You know, that's like continuing the 'Circle of Why Bother.”

"The Circle of Why Bother" is very important because it not only identifies worthless majors, but also points out why they're worthless. If the primary form of employment for a major is to simply re-teach it to future students, then there is no practical application for it outside academia. And since there is no practical application for it outside academia, it has no value.

Might be interesting.

Might be fun.

But people do not pay you a salary to do things that are fun or interesting. People do fun and interesting things for free.

All those who participate in "The Circle of Why Bother" degrees are simply little children who want to be paid to pursue a hobby and maybe teach to feign some kind of professionalism. Worse still, a lot of your tax money goes to pay for what is nothing more than other people's hobbies. Take the moral high ground, become a real adult and avoid becoming a parasite. Avoid degrees in "The Circle of Why Bother."

CHAPTER 6 “WHY DIDN'T ANYBODY TELL ME?”

Given the importance of choosing the right major a simple question arises:

“Why didn't anybody tell me?”

You would think out of all the guidance counselors, school therapists, teachers, administrators, and college recruiters at least one of them would have come out of the woodwork and told you, or at least warned you about these worthless degrees. Even more perplexing might be why your parents haven't sat you down and had a discussion with you about choosing the right major. Sadly, there is no one right answer because there is a confluence of reasons why different people didn't inform you about the realities and consequences of choosing different degrees. Some of these are innocent, such as ignorance or being uninformed themselves.

Others, however, are just plain evil and wrong. And even though it is likely by now you won't be declaring a worthless major, you still need to be informed about why nobody told you about worthless degrees because whether you know it or not, you are the biggest target for many people's nefarious plans.

Spineless Parents

Without going into a long and detailed socio-psychological analysis of the generations that came before you, you have to realize the Baby Boomers and Gen X'ers are more or less spineless. Not in all regards and instances, but when it comes to parenting, these generations are truly spineless. They're afraid to spank their children. They prefer timeouts versus genuine discipline. Instead of negative-reinforcement it's always positive reinforcement. They all want to be their "children's best friend." In short, your parents have abandoned the tough, fatherly love approach to rearing and opted instead for the nurturing, motherly love approach.

While some therapists and feminists might welcome this development, unfortunately there is a drawback to pursuing such a lopsided rearing philosophy. Not only does it fail to account for the psychology of half the population (males), it's taking the easy way out. It really is not parenting. It's refusing to face up to the harsh fact that you have to mete out punishment when the kid deserves it. You can't be "chummy buddies" with your kids all the time and need to make hard choices and hard decisions. Instead, to maintain a nice, quiet (and consequently) fake happiness among the family, parents today simply defer any harsh decisions perpetually into the future, inevitably never getting around to them.

This means you were brought up in a bubble. You weren't brought up in the real world. Your parents, who perhaps loved you "too much," didn't want you to suffer anything. Worse still, a lot of them probably led you to believe you were "great" and destined for "great things!" Not only were you destined, you deserved great things. You were entitled to success!

"Look, you shot for 3% in the basketball game son! Great job!!! You're going to become the next Michael Jordan!"

"Wow! You got 27th place in the competition! I'm so proud of you, Sweetheart!"

Unfortunately, that's not the real world. All they managed to do in shielding you from the real world and bloating your egos, was set you up for a spectacular failure in the future once the real world came crashing down on you. So, after 17 years of essentially kissing your ass, do you think they have the gall to tell you that what you chose to major in was stupid? It's not that they don't love you, they just don't know how to break it to you.

Fortunately for you, I'm not your parents. I'm the author that hopes you and millions of youth like you read this book, major in great subjects, have great and rewarding careers, and live happy and successful lives. I also, consequently, want you to be productive members of society so you contribute to my social security fund.

Worthless Guidance Counselors

Guidance counselors, be they at high school or college, are the same thing as your parents, just worse. Not only do they lack the courage to tell you the truth, they have the added benefit of being ignorant.

First, understand spinelessness doesn't just relegate itself to Baby Boomer or Gen X parents. It is a generation-wide trait. That means not only are the majority of parents spineless, that means the majority of teachers, guidance counselors, principals, professors and mentors are also spineless because they belong to the same generation. Magnifying this effect is that those who pursue degrees in education are not really your ruff and gruff fatherly types. They are more psychologically predisposed to be the touchy feely type. So if it comes time to tell you the truth about the major you just chose, do you think timid, little Ms. Nettle in the guidance office is going to say,

"What!? English!?? Are you crazy! You already speak English! Why on god's green Earth would you major in English! Are you a moron?! How much money are you going to spend on that! And my god! You'll piss away four years of your youth and have nothing to show for it! You freaking idiot, here, let me pull out this chart! You see here? Starting salaries for petroleum engineers are three times that of English majors!"

Probably not.

Second, what do you think the majority of guidance counselors majored in?

Right. Probably a worthless degree.

Not only are they spineless and would dare not tell you the truth, they don't even know what the truth is. As far as they're concerned, they majored in a worthless degree, were lucky enough to have landed a government job as a "counselor," and because it's a government job, they've never experienced any kind of job insecurity or unemployment. Matter of fact, neither have any of their co-workers. Far as they're concerned, that's a great career. The only observation they've made about the labor market is how "unfair" it is that Joe Mauer makes $280 billion/year and teachers and counselors only make $36,000/9 months.

So when it comes to your guidance counselor providing you any kind of genuine, practical guidance you can forget it simply because they don't know what they're talking about. You alone in reading chapter two of this book probably have more economic knowledge than your average guidance counselor and are infinitely wiser when it comes to choosing a worthwhile major.

The Nefarious Side of Education

As harsh a criticism as I've laid on spineless parents and naïve guidance counselors, there is one thing you cannot accuse them of and that is being evil. Your parents most likely love you and want only the best for you. Guidance counselors also want what's best for you and provide the best advice they're capable of giving. It's not like they lay awake at night, concocting evil plans on how they can screw up your future by channeling you into worthless degree programs. But just because they aren't, doesn't mean nobody else is.

Whether you believe it or not, there are nefarious forces in education actively conspiring against you. Not only do they aim to take advantage of you, they already have. You don't see it because you've been in the educational system for most of your life and thus are not extracted from it far enough to see what's happening. Additionally, the education system has this sort of "sacred" and "pure" reputation that puts it above criticism and reproach. So, if anybody dares to criticize teachers or education, or just plain has the gall to point out the truth, the accuser is vilified as somebody who "hates children" and is "against education." This not only prevents any constructive criticism of the education industry from getting through, it provides the necessary cover for these nefarious forces to continue unopposed.

This sounds like a conspiracy theory, but it really isn't. This is a fact. This is happening. Whether you choose to believe it or not is another matter, but the sooner you realize the reality of the situation, the better equipped you will be to identify those trying to take advantage of you and avoid becoming their next victim.

The Perfect Storm

First, you must understand there are three traits or "factors" that are in play that makes education a very attractive environment for charlatans or outright crooks. The first factor is again the untouchable reputation "education" has in today's society. Education is "holy." It's "pure." It's for the "children." It's "our future."

And, for the most part, they're right. Education is vital. Education is absolutely necessary. The reason why is that education is what makes a country grow and thrive. If you have an educated work force, not only are they more productive, they are more innovative. They can produce more for less, driving down the cost of goods and increasing people's standards of living. Educated people also create new and innovative things that cure cancer, play MP3's, provide us with limitless energy, and a whole host of other financial, social, health, recreational and environmental benefits. If it weren't for education we would quite literally still be living in caves trying to invent the wheel.

But because of how vital it is, education gets a pass when it comes to any form of criticism or audit. Nobody is allowed to criticize it. Nobody is allowed to judge it. Because of this, education, no matter how important it is to society, is not watched over or guarded closely to make sure charlatans do not invade it, corrupt it, and turn it towards their own selfish purposes.

The second trait confirms the first one in terms of just how much we value education. No doubt in school you've been told about how evil "Big Oil" is, right? And how "they don't pay their fair share?" And how "the entire industry is corrupt?" Certainly, if we just spent as much money on education as we did "Big Oil" then all would be right with the world.

Right?

Well guess again, kiddos. Despite what you were "told" in school, we spend nearly three times the amount of money on education than we do the entire oil, gas and energy industries. In 2010 over $1 trillion was spent on education in the US, compared to just $354 billion on

"Big Oil." We even spend more on education than we do the entire US military budget, which amounted to "only" $685 billion in 2010.

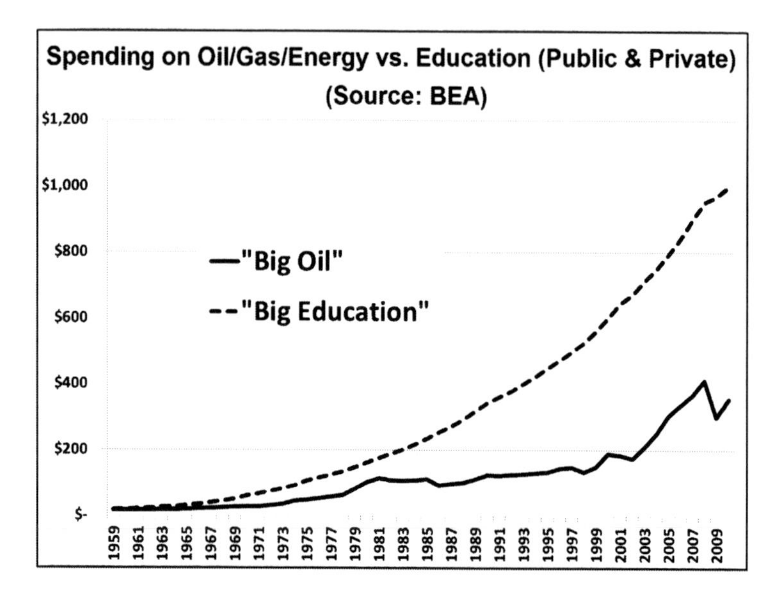

Now, if you think "evil" industries like "Big Oil" and the "Industrial Military Complex" are corrupt with their billions of dollars, do you think there's any chance there might be some corruption in the $1 trillion education industry? I mean, nobody looks at that $1 trillion per year in education spending and thinks to take advantage of it right? And given the government accounts for over 75% of that spending, there's absolutely no way there could be any corruption in the industry, right?

No, of course not, “Big Education” is pure as the virgin snow.

The third and final trait is to ask what kind of people does education attract, or more specifically, what kind of quality and caliber of people does education employ? To answer that we just need to look at the two generations that currently populate the education industry – the Baby Boomers and Gen X.

Smart as you may think you are, you aren’t the only one to come up with the genius diabolical plot to major in a cake subject and then somehow hope you land some kind of easy, government, non-profit type job. Matter of fact, two entire generations before you came up with that exact same idea! Millions of people before you also majored in Philosophy, Women’s Studies, Communications, English and all the other worthless degrees. Where do you suppose they ended up?

Not in the fluid dynamics department at your local oil refining firm.

Not in the tax department at your local accountancy.

Certainly not in the neurosurgery department at your local hospital.

Surprise, surprise, they ended up in education!

Why did they end up there? Because nobody else would have them. Naturally, the only place they could go was academia because it doesn't take any real skill or talent to teach. I don't care how many people that insults, because it's true. Teaching is easy. Anybody who claims otherwise hasn't worked a real job in their life before. But opinions of the rigors of teaching aside, the main point is the talent pool most educators were pulled from was the talentless. Congratulations, the "vital" education industry is headed up by those who can't do, but can only teach.

The larger point of this third trait, however, is to realize what the primary incentive was for today's educators to go into education. Though there are some who did indeed love children and genuinely cared about educating future generations, the majority of "teachers" or "professors" didn't go into education in the hopes someday they'd be able to educate you. They went into education first and foremost for themselves, the primary reason being it's the only industry that would have them. Educating you was merely an afterthought, if not an inconvenient chore that was required to get a check.

Teachers > Students

When you combine the three traits together you now see the scam that is being perpetuated upon the youth. The primary purpose of "Big Education" is nothing as noble or honorable as educating the precious, little children. Its primary function is that of an employment vehicle for people who are otherwise unemployable.

Of course, this is quite a damning accusation I've made against the entire industry. And no doubt this goes against what you were told in school. But, like the chart above probably proved you were misinformed about "Big Oil," perhaps you may have been misinformed or outright lied to about other things. Not that I'm planning on fully convincing you in these few short chapters (that will be up to you and your intellectual honesty if you care to research this at further length), but perhaps some additional data and statistics may at least get you to start questioning what you've been told and daring to have an independent thought. Enough independent thought to give you some street smarts so you can avoid being taken advantage of by "Big Education."

More Money = Better Education

An outstanding opportunity to teach you some street smarts is to look at the age-old claim that "more money equals better education." Not a year goes by where your public school doesn't come to the taxpayer (i.e.- your parents) with a cup in their hand and demand more money. The logic being the more money you spend on a school, the better the education those kids will receive. And who doesn't want a better education for the little children?

Logically, this stands to reason. More money should afford more teachers, more books, better equipment, resulting in an overall better school with better educational outcomes. And so we all just accept the premise that more money equals better education.

But do you know that for a fact?

Have you looked it up?

How do you know?

Thankfully, I looked it up for you.

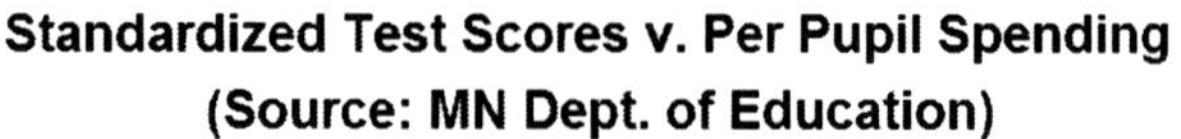

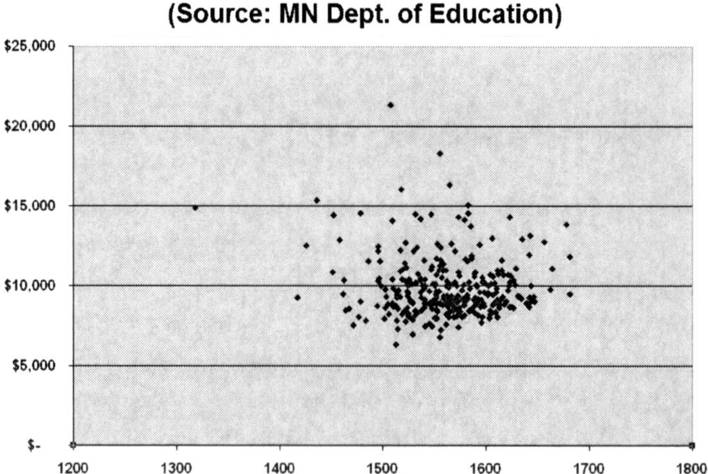

You'll notice there is no correlation between spending per pupil and standardized test scores (at least in Minnesota). Matter of fact, there's a slight negative correlation. Regardless, the question is, why would they lie to you like that? Why would they continue to claim that more money equals better schools when it's just not true? Well, there are two theories.

One, the entire education industry is oblivious to this. Out of the trillion dollars they receive annually they've not the resources to pull together the data and recreate the chart I did above. Matter of fact, it never occurred to them. They're just so gosh darn busy educating you precious little kids.

Or, two, the teachers union and public schools are putting themselves and their revenue stream ahead of educating the children. The money is more important to them and so they don't really care what the reality is, they will just keep citing "more money equals better schools" because it gets them more funding. Matter of fact, they'll go so far as to abuse the children by holding them hostage demanding, "give us more money or the kid gets it," compelling parents to fork over more money for a new and unnecessary "gym teacher" or "social worker."

Again, you don't have to believe me. But if you want to do some research, you could start by looking up some videos online of all the "selfless" teachers that left their "precious students" in the classroom to go protest in Madison, Wisconsin in 2011.

Prerequisites

Another bit of evidence that there are indeed people aiming to take advantage of you in the education industry is "prerequisites." K-12 education is one thing, but college is another. For the most part, your teachers in elementary school through high school care a lot more about you than your average college professor. But because of the sheer volume of dollars being spent on college degrees, universities have come up with ever more clever and witty ways to extract more money from you. One of the more prominent ones being "prerequisites."

Prerequisites are classes that have nothing to do with your major, will not help you graduate any sooner, and will do absolutely nothing to help you in your career. But they are required because those loving caring college administrators want you to be (are you ready for it?)

"Well rounded."

This is complete, BS.

The real reason they make you take prerequisites is to generate more money for other departments, notably departments of worthless majors. In short, you are paying to create make-work jobs for graduate students who just plain cannot find a job outside of "Big Education." You are also helping complete "The Circle of Why Bother." Understand worthless degree programs are like zombies. They always need new bodies to enter the program, otherwise the program goes away. So to ensure there's enough demand to keep these worthless programs going, they force all of you non-worthless degree people to take some token class in those fields.

But what really exposes the nefarious side of education is the sheer number of prerequisites the average college student is forced to take. It's not like you take one or two prerequisites and then you're done. Oh, no, not by a long shot. If you look at any undergraduate degree you'll see nearly half of your classes have nothing to do with your major. Worst still, the costs of these prerequisites are not just the thousands of dollars in unnecessary tuition added to your bill, but the opportunity costs of having to take these pointless classes. Not only could you literally graduate in two years with a bachelor's degree and be just as capable if you didn't have to take prerequisites, imagine how much better of an accountant or an engineer you would be upon graduation if all of your classes were in your major.

Again, you'll probably just dismiss me as an old curmudgeon, angry at the world and just wanting to ruin everybody's good time with my "crazy conspiracy theories." Just smile when you cut the check for all those prerequisites you'll never use.

Tuition Costs

What I love more than anything else is when college students protest increases in tuition. They usually go to the state capitol and protest that the government is not spending enough on education. But like pretty much every protestor in the history of protesting, not one of them bothered to look up the state budget or university budget to actually inform themselves as to why tuition is going up. That would take too much effort.

But here's a question. If the chart from before shows money spent on education skyrocketing and the majority of that money coming from the government, why are tuition prices constantly going up at a rate faster than inflation? Shouldn't all that money be subsidizing tuition prices? Perhaps another chart can answer. Below is a chart that shows you how much inflation there has been in three things:

- Average tuition costs
- The U of MN Presidents' salaries
- The CPI which measures inflation

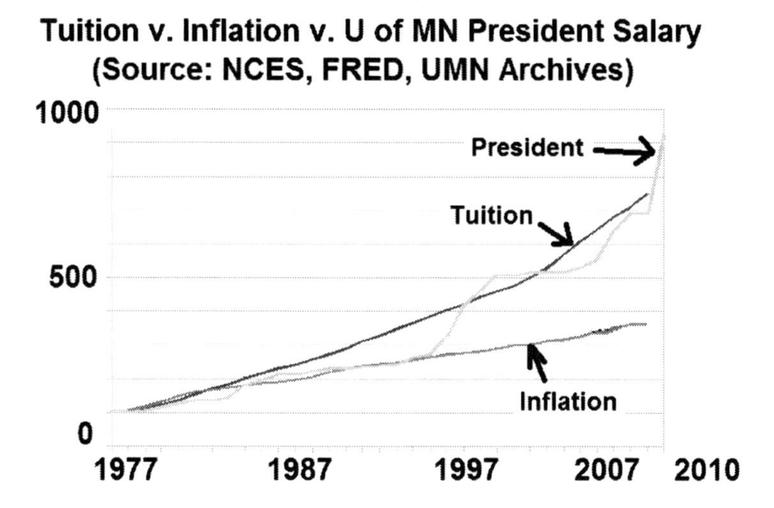

What's great about this chart is it shows you the real reason tuition is going up. It's not that the government isn't spending enough, it's that all the money goes to pay skyrocketing salaries. Additionally, it's not just people's salaries that are going up at colleges, but the sheer number of people they employ. If you care to be intellectually honest, you can always go and look up any university's budget and see how much they spend on salaries as well as how many people they employ.

Of course, this chart behooves another question. When all those college kids are protesting against increases in tuition costs and blaming the government for not spending enough, are all the deans and presidents and administrators just laughing at the spectacular ignorance of the students? I mean, they must really get a kick out of watching thousands of students blame the taxpayer for being stingy while they're bringing down a $600,000 salary with $200,000 in bonuses and passing the costs onto your tuition bill. But no, no. They're not taking advantage of you. It's still all just a conspiracy theory on my part.

The Profitability of Worthless Degrees

Profitability and worthless degrees rarely go together. However, there is an inordinate amount of profit to be had in worthless degrees, specifically for the colleges offering them.

If you think about it, which degrees produce the most profit for universities and colleges? If you look at engineering, science, bio-medical, computer and other STEM fields, to teach these subjects you effectively need to spend a lot of money on equipment and hardware. I remember, quite clearly, entire rooms of servers and super-computers at the Computer Science Building back in my college days and wondering how much they cost. Combine those costs with how few students actually major in those subjects and you can see these degrees have a lot of expenses, but limited revenue.

Contrast that with the “start-up costs” of offering a communications program, an MBA program, or a law school. All you need in those cases is a classroom, some tables and chairs, and a washed up, unemployed professor. Furthermore, consider the considerably higher volume of students pursuing these easier classes. And even more than that, you can charge twice as much for an advanced program like an MBA or law degree.

Obviously, colleges and universities have a huge financial incentive to push the liberal arts, the humanities, and worthless grad schools because of the profits they generate. It doesn't matter that none of these degrees are going to help you in your future employment endeavors. That's not their concern. They already got your money.

CHAPTER 7
DEBUNKING MYTHS

As you enter college you will be entering a new world that you are unfamiliar with. Additionally, this will be the first time most of you are truly on your own. Not that you don't have familial support, or the advice of your father isn't a phone call away, but you are now officially an adult and able to make your own decisions, for better or worse. You are also officially a noob at being an adult, which makes you an easy mark for those wishing to take advantage of you.

For example, credit card companies love noob adults because they are prone to rack up tons up debt and pay tons of interest. I guarantee you that there will be credit card companies setting up tables and kiosks on campus when you start your freshman year. Employers also love noob adults because they can promise you a job with experience, only to have you do the filing and faxing nobody else wants to do. Car salesman love you noob adults too, selling you cars you just plain can't afford. But, as was alluded to in previous chapters, there are adults in the education industry who also wouldn't mind preying off of you as well. So, when you get to college, who do you trust or seek for advice? Who do you believe and listen to? And who do you tell to go jump in a lake?

Obviously, you will not be able to tell an honest professor who genuinely cares about helping you advance your career from that of a charlatan, life-long, "Big Education" careerist. Nobody wears name tags saying,

"Hello, I'm one of the good, honest people here to help you."

Just as you won't see,

"Hi, I'm from the nefarious dark side, give me your money."

But, there are some myths, falsehoods and just outright lies people will tell you that will give them away. Not that in knowing these myths you will be able to avoid paying for prerequisite classes, but it will identify which people you can trust, what kind of extra-curricular activities are worthwhile, which classes or departments are worthwhile, and which classes and majors to avoid, making your college experience easier and more productive.

Myth #1 - "You Need to Be Well Rounded"

I find this canard particularly condescending because it implies you are a boring, incapable, uninteresting person. That you just go to school, study, and then go home. You have no friends, you have no interests, you have no hobbies. Therefore, you are in desperate need of a score of expensive prerequisite classes to give you that culture and well-roundedness that only an overpaid, blowhard, pony-tail-wearing professor can give you.

When conducting seminars on worthless degrees, I usually point to three or four students and ask them one simple question:

"What do you like to do in your free time?"

And what's amazing is how many young people are not boring, uninteresting, incapable people without a hobby or an interest. I've meet scores of very interesting students. Students who play guitar, go rock climbing, are amateur chefs at home. Students who like to fish, like to hunt, or just like to practice marksmanship. I met one student who builds go-karts with his father. I met another who likes to make her own jewelry.

How can it be these young kids are so interesting without the benefit of having all those prerequisites to make them "well-rounded?!"

Obviously, you are all already well-rounded. You have interests, you have hobbies, and the proof you're well-rounded is that you have friends. In reality, you don't need classes to be "well-rounded." It's just another scam to extract money from you.

Myth #2 - "It's Not All About Money!"

Yes it is.

Don't let anybody tell you otherwise. There are three major reasons it is about the money whether you want it to be or not.

One, unless you are rich or come from a rich family, you are going to college, whether you like it or not, to increase your employability. At the age of 18 you do not have the luxury of doing things that "aren't for money." Those are called hobbies. You can pursue hobbies when you move out of your parents' basement, put food on the table, clothe yourself, and put a shelter over your head. Quit being an idealistic moron who can't afford it, set down the peace drums, grow up and hit the books.

Two, if you spend $50,000 on tuition it damn well better be about the money. In dropping that much coin on a degree, you've now forced a serious financial consequence to it. Furthermore, there really is a hypocrisy to those who spend money on a degree, but still claim it isn't about the money. The reason is the majority of these people are pursuing worthless degrees, but most of these degrees can be self-taught, behooving the question,

"If you can do it for free, and you're doing it for purely intellectual purposes, why are you paying for it?"

The answer is that deep down inside they're not doing it for purely intellectual purposes. They believe (or perhaps "hope" is a better word) that there will be a financial return in the end.

Three, anybody telling you this is most likely the one who will be receiving your money when you part with it.

Myth #3 – "Congratulations, You Made It to the Dean's List!"

In order to make it to the honor roll or "dean's list" you need to achieve a certain GPA. The GPA varies from school to school, but the rule of thumb is you need a 3.0 or higher. Unfortunately, today to get a job you need something more like a 3.5 or higher. The reason why is grade inflation.

As the spinelessness continued to infect the education industry, standards of rigor went out the window. Now afraid to hurt your feelings, schools from kindergarten to college have lowered their standards to make it so that everybody gets B's. We've eliminated scoring from school sports and some schools have done away with the honor roll altogether. While that may have caused warm-fuzzies in everybody's stomach at school and "everybody's a winner," employers knew better. Employers got to hire all these "honor roll students" whose skills proved to be more of the C-, D+ variety. Don't let your grades or your professors fool you. You need to achieve a 3.5 or better, unless it is in a really rigorous course of study. Employers have adjusted for grade inflation.

On a related note, you will find more and more colleges requiring some sort of extra-curricular activity in order to be put on the official dean's list. I had a 3.96, but still didn't graduate with honors because I did not participate in these extra-curricular activities. These extra-curricular activities are, frankly, nothing more than further political indoctrination that's been foisted upon you in school already. Back in my day, I had to spend a full week on four different categories – diversity, environment, social responsibility and some other such communist-themed category – in order to graduate with "honors." I can only imagine what the requirements are now.

Don't waste your time with these hoops. If you get a 4.0, the employer won't care if you officially graduated with "honors." As far as they're concerned you did.

Myth #4 – "A Bachelor's Degree is Just to Get in the Door"

You will often hear people say,

"It doesn't matter what your degree is in, it's what you do with it."

or

"Employers don't really care what your degree is in, just that you completed it."

Whatever the variant of this myth, there was some truth to it in the past. Completing college was quite an achievement and only a minority of people did so. However, today graduating from college is no big deal. Standards have been lowered and the universities are flooded with worthless degrees. For the most part, people just use college as a party experience instead of one to hone a skill or a trade.

Today when you hear somebody say the degree doesn't matter, it's usually just a liberal arts major telling himself what he wants to hear or liberal arts graduates rationalizing why they aren't working in the field they studied. Understand, it definitely does matter what your degree is in. If it didn't matter, then all majors would have the exact same starting salaries and employment prospects.

Myth #5 – "Employers Value Critical Thinking and Communication Skills"

"Critical thinking" is a term you'll run into in the liberal arts and humanities. In short, it is the ability to be intellectually honest and get to the bottom of things, i.e.-discover the truth. Now they complicate things by making it horribly complex, prescribing processes and procedures to practice critical thinking, even writing entire books on critical thinking. But in the end it's just the ability to sit down, think things through, and get to the bottom of things.

Communications is, of course, simply the ability to communicate. Everybody has this skill, despite what doctorates in Communications would suggest.

Now these two skills, critical thinking and the ability to communicate, everybody has. Whether you knew the official term "critical thinking" doesn't matter, because at one point in time in all of our lives we've had to sit down, analyze a situation and get to the bottom of it. Also, after 18 years of speaking and writing the same language, I believe we're all on the same page when it comes to communication skills. However, we have an added benefit over even the most advanced doctorates in Communications and the world's most critical thinkers:

We're sane.

Understand somebody who has dedicated eight years of collegiate study to simple concepts like "communications" or "critical thinking" is quite literally insane. Normal people just accept minor skills such as reason, logic and language as a given. Matter of fact, most of us never gave these things a thought as they are so instinctual and natural. But, insane people go and get doctorates in these simple concepts, write 900 page textbooks about them, while forcing their students to buy said books.

Now, what is bound to happen when you're forced to take your prerequisites is you are going to run into one of these professors who dedicated a significant amount of their youth studying simple concepts like communications and critical thinking skills. And while you may think it's foolish, you must realize this person has spent his entire professional career in academia, not in the real world. In other words, they've been living in a bubble and because of this, they actually think skills like "communications" or "critical thinking" are high-end, cutting edge skills. When in reality it's like when your dog found some two year old decayed rabbit carcass and brought it home and was all proud of it. Or how a two year old finally goes to the bathroom in the toilet for the first time and drags you to the toilet bowl to show you. That's how communications doctorates are. They're enormously impressed with themselves while nobody else is because what's there to be impressed about?

But since that's all they know, that's what they think is in demand in the real world. So when they are asked about the real world practical applications of a liberal arts degree, without fail they say,

"Employers appreciate liberal art students because of their communication and critical thinking skills."

Which is like saying employers appreciate that you are potty-trained and know how to bathe.

Just be wary of those peddling "critical thinking" or "communications" as skills.

Myth #6 - Median and Mean Income

You'll often hear college recruiters or guidance counselors stress the importance of at minimum getting a bachelors degree. To make their point they'll cite some simple statistics, notably how much more your lifetime earnings will be over a high school graduate, as well as the average salary of a college graduate compared to somebody with just their high school diploma.

What they fail to tell you is how this data is skewed due to a handful of bachelor graduates moving on and making millions, if not, billions of dollars. This brings up the mean average and unless you are the next Steve Jobs, you are unlikely to ever realize this kind of earnings potential. As of 2010, the mean average salary of a person with a bachelor's degree was $56,740. The median (which is what most of us are likely to make) was only $43,143. Notice, once again, plumbers or other tradesmen make more for half the education.

Myth #7 – "You Should Get an Internship"

Internships are merely a way for companies to sucker cheap, if not, free labor out of you. The company will dangle the chance to get "real world experience" in front of you, maybe even some token amount of pay, and you will be suckered in to go and do glamorous things such as filing, data entry and other secretarial work.

That is not to say that all internships are like that. There are the rare and occasional internships where you are actually learning something vital and helpful to your career. These internships are more centered around STEM degrees because of the specialized skill required to do work in those fields. But even in STEM and certainly in business fields, you can expect the majority of internships to merely be a low end job where your primary purpose is to do all the crap work nobody else wants to do.

Despite all this you should try to get one internship under your belt. But do so according to the following rules:

- The nanosecond you realize the majority of your work is merely to do filing, faxing, scanning, etc., leave. Don't tell them, don't inform them. Leave. Also, file a complaint with that company's HR department and inform the career services center of your college about the false advertising of that firm.
- Keep trying to find an internship that does give you experience. This may take three or four tries, but inevitably you will find one that is worthwhile.
- Do not spend more than six months at an internship. Get it on your resume, establish a good rapport with your boss, but then cite college as your primary responsibility. Only if they offer you full-time employment after graduation should you stick around.
- Only get one internship. Additional internships add nothing to your marketability. Spend your time instead drinking, chasing girls/boys and playing volleyball.

Myth #7 - Women and the Wage Gap

Without going into a long and boring political diatribe, the nefarious forces of "Big Education" target not just young noob adults entering college, they also like to target sub-segments of the population in a "divide and conquer" sort of way. Specifically, they like to target women.

Because of this you have a whole host of myths specifically perpetrated upon women in college. I ask that you women reading these myths please set your ideological leanings aside and just merely listen. The reason is that I am not trying to convince you of any political ideology, I'm just plain trying to make your collegiate experience more enjoyable and productive by pointing out the truth. You don't have to believe me, you don't have to like me, all I ask is that you give what I say a token amount of thought.

Depending on the source you cite, women make only 76% of what men do. They call this the "wage gap." This "wage gap" will constantly be pounded into your skulls while you attend college and will be cited to constantly remind you about how oppressed you poor women are and how lucky you men have it.

It's about the most damaging lie ever told to women.

The reason it's so damaging to women is because it suggests that it's ***outside your control to close that 24% gap***. Think about it. If it's really the big, bad, sexist men holding you down and oppressing you, then there's not much you can do about it. You just have to suffer it. So what do women do? They go about their business, major in what they want, and just chalk that gap up to sexism.

However, it is within the control of women to close this gap because the wage gap is not caused by "sexism" or "evil, big, bad, meanie men." It's caused primarily by a disproportionate percentage of women choosing worthless degrees.

Nearly 70% of worthless degrees are awarded to women.

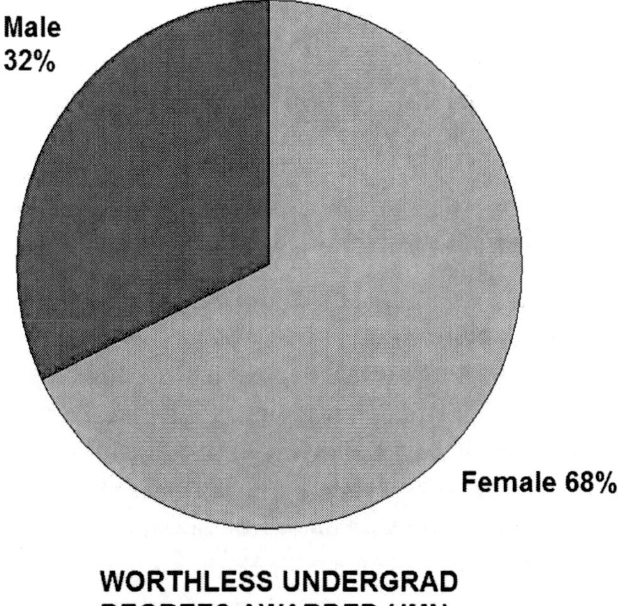

WORTHLESS UNDERGRAD DEGREES AWARDED UMN (Source: UMN)

Worse, only 1 in 5 engineering degrees go to women.

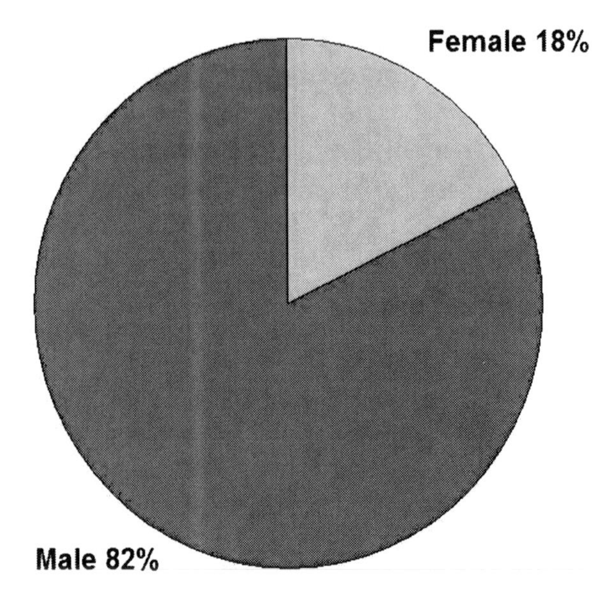

ENGINEERING DEGREES UMN
(Source: UMN)

This is not an opinion. This is not a piece of political propaganda. This is just the sad, plain truth. However, there is no better example in the saying "the truth shall set you free." Instead of wallowing in self-pity and thinking the situation is hopeless, these charts should be some of the most welcomed news to women because they are liberating you from the myth that you can't do anything about it. These charts prove you are not oppressed, you are not under the thumb of a bunch of misogynistic men, you have the exact same opportunities as men do and will enjoy the exact same benefits as men do. Nobody is holding you back...well...except for "Big Education" telling you to follow your heart and get a degree in Puppies and Unicorns.

Do not listen to people who say girls can't do engineering or STEM degrees. Do not listen to people who say "girls aren't good at math" (especially when you tell yourself that). You can do it. Women before you have done it. And besides, with a ratio of four guys to every girl in engineering, you'll never go without a date.

Myth #8 – "Women Earn the Majority of Degrees"

This is not a myth. It is true. Women today earn the majority of degrees. In 2010, 57% of the bachelor's degrees were awarded to women, 59% of the masters degrees were awarded to women, and for the first time in history women earned half of all PhD's.

There's just one problem.

In what?

Engineering? Neuroscience? Accounting? Econometrics? The stuff the villagers want?

Or was it English? Child Psychology? Anthropology? Chocolates and Ice Cream?

As evidenced by the charts above, it was more the Literature, Music, Unicorn Breeding variety of degrees.

Do not let this myth artificially bolster your ego. Additionally, for men, do not let this depress you either. It doesn't matter if you are male or female, it matters what you major in and what you produce in the end. Such statistics are nothing more than a distraction from what really matters.

Myth #9 – "1 in 3 College Women are Sexually Assaulted"

Though this has nothing to do with your employment prospects or future career, I do want you to have an enjoyable social life in college. One of the biggest impediments to this is the statistic of how many women are sexually assaulted on college campuses.

Upon moving into your dorm, most colleges and universities will have a brain-washing session that is disguised as "freshman orientation." Among the propaganda will be the token statistic of "*1 in 3 women are sexually assaulted on campus*." It could be 1 in 4, or 1 in 5 depending on the mood of the feminists on campus at the time, but it ultimately doesn't matter because this is a lie that hurts women more than helps them. The reason why is it scares young women away from dating, hanging out with men and developing healthy, normal relationships with men.

Realize these statistics are created by the women's studies departments on campus to maintain a "victim" status of women. This victim status begets not just pity, but usually funding and additional financial resources to their programs. A "sexual abuse center" or "shelter" is usually set up on campus, not primarily for genuine victims of sexual assault, but rather to create jobs for otherwise unemployable women's studies majors. Worse still, in order to receive additional funding, these feminists will lower the bar in terms of what constitutes "sexual assault" on campus to include innocuous things like an unwanted advance from a guy, thereby making it seem there's an "epidemic" of sexual assault on campus.

Aside from ruining the relations between men and women on campus, as well as making men walk on eggshells in fear of being accused of a sexual crime, such fabricated statistics scare women away from any kind of dating or social engagement with men. Dating, however, is supposed to be one of the biggest fringe benefits of college (and for a lot of guys I knew it was their primary reason they attended college). But, because of the nefarious forces of "Big Education," young freshmen are merely used as pawns in what is nothing more than a political game, and suffer a lesser college experience for it.

If you really want to know the statistics of sexual assault on campus, don't go to the women's studies department, go to the police department. The police will not only have the real statistics on sexual assault, but reports on crime, trends, statistics, what areas of town to avoid, escort programs and other practical, helpful safety tips.

CHAPTER 8
THE MORAL IMPORTANCE OF CHOOSING THE RIGHT MAJOR

Your Moral Responsibility to Society

You have two responsibilities in this world. To society and to yourself.

Your responsibility to society is quite simple. You don't live off of it and you carry your own weight. You produce something of value, earn a living, support yourself and anybody you bring into this world, and hopefully, upon your demise, you've contributed more than you consumed thereby avoiding becoming a parasite, as well as earning the title "contributing member of society." This means making wise decisions like getting insurance and saving enough up for retirement, spending within your means, and not having kids you can't afford. But underpinning all of this is finding employment that can support you and your lifestyle which means, once again, you have to choose the right major.

On the onset, you may ask the question,

"Well, as long as I have a job, then I'm producing something of value and supporting myself, right?"

But, we have to revisit out little village analogy because having a job doesn't necessarily mean you are producing something the village wants or needs. Matter of fact, you'll find a significant amount of jobs not only produce nothing of value, they drain resources from jobs that do.

The perfect example of "productionless jobs" are the fine men and women employed in "The Circle of Why Bother." We alluded to this before, but the basic point is that if the only practical application of a worthless degree is to become a professor and simply re-teach it to future students, then it has no value. There are no practical applications or uses of these degrees outside academia, so all the millions of people spending billions of hours on "The Circle of Why Bother" are simply wasting their time. However, it isn't just their time they are wasting. It would be wonderful if that was the case, but sadly it is not.

If people in "The Circle of Why Bother" are not producing anything of value to society, how do they eat?

How do they pay rent? How do they sustain themselves? The answer is simple – you pay for it. You'll notice a lot of people employed in "The Circle of Why Bother" industry are employed at public universities and colleges. This means you, and all the other taxpayers out there, pay for these people to essentially have careers in what is nothing more than a worthless hobby. Even if it is a private school, your tax dollars via government student loan programs to the students who major in this tripe, still go to pay for these people's hobbies.

When this inconvenient truth is pointed out and members of "The Circle" realize their funding, and therefore, cushy lifestyle is being threatened, they will immediately become indignant and vigorously defend the merit of their discipline. It is here you will hear things like "we're raising awareness" or "helping the children." Also, in nearly 99% of the instances, they've managed to interweave their program with some kind of noble political crusade such as "fighting poverty" or "global warming." They do this so when you criticize their program for not doing anything, then they can claim you "hate the children" or "hate the environment." Whatever ballyhoo and hubbub they throw up, these are merely tactics and euphemisms used to hide the truth. And that truth is these people are nothing more than economic parasites. They produce nothing of value for society and expect society to pay for their make-believe "careers."

Another area you will see "productionless jobs" is in the non-profit or charity industries. What makes this group particularly insipid is not how they're genuinely economically parasitic, but how they usually champion some noble crusade to extract money from others to support their "career." The UN is a grand example. If you look at the UN and all of its varied charitable subdivisions (UNICEF, UNAID, etc.) it is a spectacular failure. Matter of fact, if you look at all charitable organizations dedicated to the "eradication of third world hunger" or the "eradication of child poverty" they have all failed miserably.

Naïve people will sit there, scratch their heads and say,

"How, with the trillions of dollars we spent on these charitable organizations, is there still hunger and poverty? Well, I guess we just need to spend another trillion dollars!"

While people with half a brain will simply realize the UN is nothing more than a larger, multi-billion dollar variation of "The Circle of Why Bother." Its primary purpose is not to eradicate AIDS or hunger or help the children. Its primary purpose is to provide employment to thousands of people with worthless degrees. If you don't believe it, just ask yourself two questions:

1. Why, with the trillions of dollars that has been spent on it, hasn't there been a marked improvement in the entire continent of Africa?
2. What does the average UN worker have a degree in?

Something tells me there aren't a lot of CPA's working at UNICEF.

An example of jobs that are not only "productionless," but actually harm the creation of other jobs are political activism jobs. Political activism, again, does not employ a lot of engineers or doctors. Additionally, because of its nature, it has that common theme of bogusly championing some altruistic crusade or another which they can hide behind should they ever be criticized. These jobs vary across political intent and scope, but the most damaging ones are centralized around "environmentalism." Two perfect examples are the shutting down of the Keystone XL pipeline in Nebraska and the St. Croix bridge in Minnesota. Neither of these may sound familiar to you, but they perfectly highlight instances where productionless people cost other people jobs.

In the case of the Keystone XL pipeline, a bunch of environmentalists managed to delay this multi-billion dollar oil pipeline from being built in Nebraska and other parts of the US. The project would have delivered some much-needed jobs during the Great Recession, not to mention bring down the price of gas for all Americans.

But a handful of environmentalists, citing the "noble cause" of the "environment" and "global warming" built up enough political influence to postpone it indefinitely. In the case of the St. Croix bridge, this is a much-needed bridge that has been in the proposal stage for the past 15 years. Its main intent is to alleviate congestion in the north east Twin Cities metro by building a bridge over the St. Croix River. Of course, the local chapter of the Sierra Club has managed time and time again to stop its construction. Not only has this cost the local economy some construction jobs, it also forces progressively longer commutes on millions of people every year (not to mention increase greenhouse gases as millions of cars just sit on the old road).

Ask yourself honestly.

Do you really think the environmentalists in Nebraska are engineers and doctors genuinely concerned about the environment? Just as the Sierra club members are hard-working electricians and auto-mechanics concerned about the St. Croix River? Of course not.

If you look up their profiles you'll see not one of them have a productive, practical degree, let alone a productive, practical job. My all-time favorite degree is held by a member of the Northstar Sierra Club Chapter who holds a "Masters in Outdoor Recreation" (I prefer to call it a "Masters in Camping"). Whatever the case, you must understand the arrogance and greed of these people. It wasn't bad enough that these people had no intention of ever becoming productive members of society, evidenced by them choosing such worthless majors. They had to go one step further and deny other people real jobs with real production value just so they could feel good about themselves. Worse still, is how they have no problem holding all of society back as they championed some kind of faux political crusade. Low gas prices, more jobs, shorter commute times, and increased standards of living for thousands be damned. Their egos are more important than the financial and economic well-being of everybody else in society. You do not have to sink to their level. You can choose instead to major in something productive and helpful to society.

And finally, there is one last category of productionless jobs, or actually, productionless people.

Politicians.

If you majored in a worthless subject and have no real skills, you inevitably either end up working in education, for a non-profit or you go to law school. However, if your parents have money, you do something different. You run for public office. To confirm my hunch, in 2009 I tallied up all the members of the Minnesota State Legislature and broke them down by whether they had a real degree or a worthless degree. The results were not surprising.

CATEGORIZED DEGREES OF MN STATE LEGISLATURE (Source: MN Legislature)

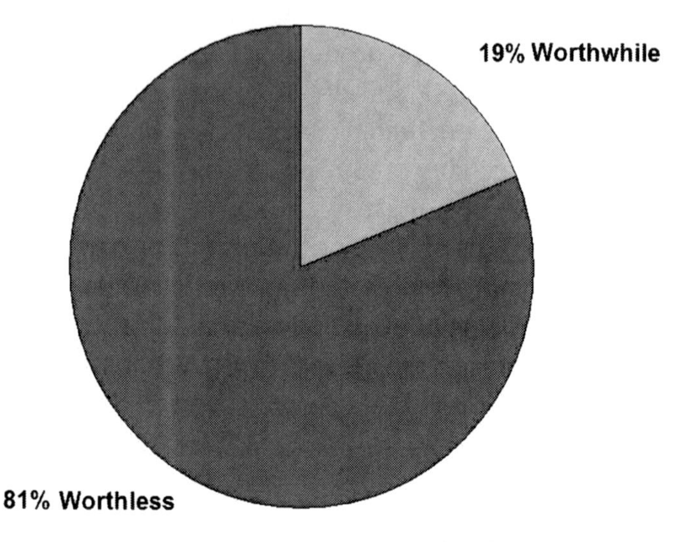

This single chart is actually worth more than a Doctorate in Political Science because it goes a long way in why you have bad government. It also reiterates the responsibility you have to society. It's obvious none of these politicians (or very few of them) are true statesmen, interested in the well-being of their constituents. They're there, first and foremost, in it for themselves. They don't really care about the people, they just couldn't find real jobs. Thankfully, their parents had a lot of money, epitomized by Minnesota's current governor, so they could run for office.

The larger point is whatever worthless degree somebody inevitably chooses, ultimately it is nothing more than an admission of laziness. Declaring a worthless major is simply shouting out to the world,

"I'm a parasite and have no intentions of working for a living. I want to do what I want to do and I want the rest of you to pay for it. I ultimately want to produce nothing society wants, but in return I demand other people slave away to make me MP3 players, computers, video games, as well as engineer hybrid cars and whatever else I want. I also want society to create some make-work job for me so my ego isn't bruised and I can make-believe I'm a real-word-live adult too. And if you dare point out what I'm doing in the real world is nothing more than parasiting off of others, I'll cowardly hide myself behind some altruistic crusade and accuse you of being a racist, a misogynist, or a hater of children."

In the end, you may be covered and disguised with a plethora of degrees and certifications. You may have a resume that is quite impressive, citing 10 years of "raising awareness experience" for one bogus cause or another. You could have the title "director" of some worthless non-profit. But in the end, you are still living off of society. You're not an adult. You're not independent. You are merely a parasite and everybody knows it.

Economic Consequences to Worthless Degrees

What's really cute, is for those of you who think you'll sneak through and land some cushy government or non-profit job, sorry to break it to you, those days are over. The reason is that you can't have three generations of people all majoring in "Cake Frosting" or "Unicorn Breeding" and expect the economy, let alone the country, to continue producing the wealth necessary to subsidize the loafers. In the end, there has to be some genuine economic production or there will be serious economic consequences. One of these consequences is probably at the forefront of a lot of young people's minds and that is unemployment.

Whether you went to college to increase your employability, or you lied to yourself and claimed you went for "intellectual purposes," today's dire labor market is in part brought to you by generations of people before you who thought they could do the exact same thing.

Unemployment, as it stands, is currently in its second worst state since the Great Depression. Though unemployment peaked at a higher level during the early 80's, the long term trend of unemployment officially categorizes this recession as the worst since 1929. You can tell yourself all you want about how your "Environmental Engineering Degree" is going to land you a job in the "green industry," but that's as likely as me meeting Jennifer Aniston in a state of desperation.

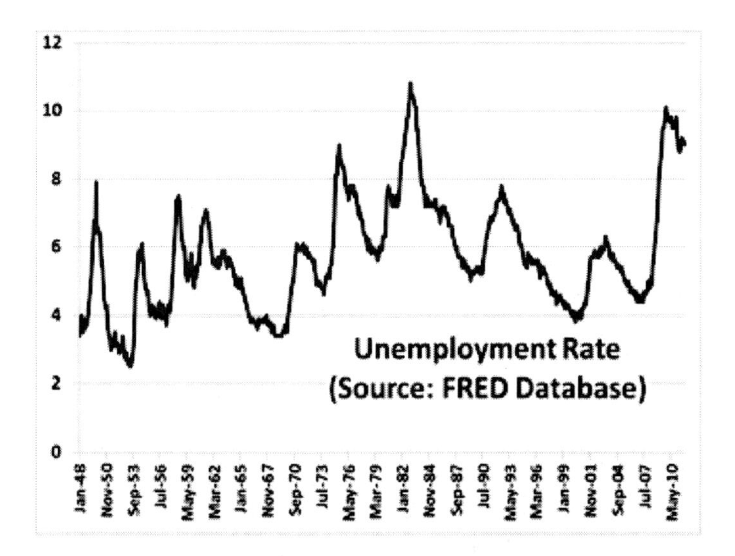

What's worse for you young people is that the unemployment rate isn't even what you should really be worried about. What you should really be concerned about is the UNDERemployment rate as it speaks to precisely why you went to college. The underemployment rate is the percent of people who are not working at their full potential. So, if you went to college for accounting, but end up working as a bartender you are considered "underemployed." The statistics vary, but the best official estimate (called U6) shows an underemployment rate considerably higher than the simple unemployment rate. Even worse than that, underemployment is typically higher in the 19-29 year old range, which means it's even more likely you will not realize the full benefit of your degree.

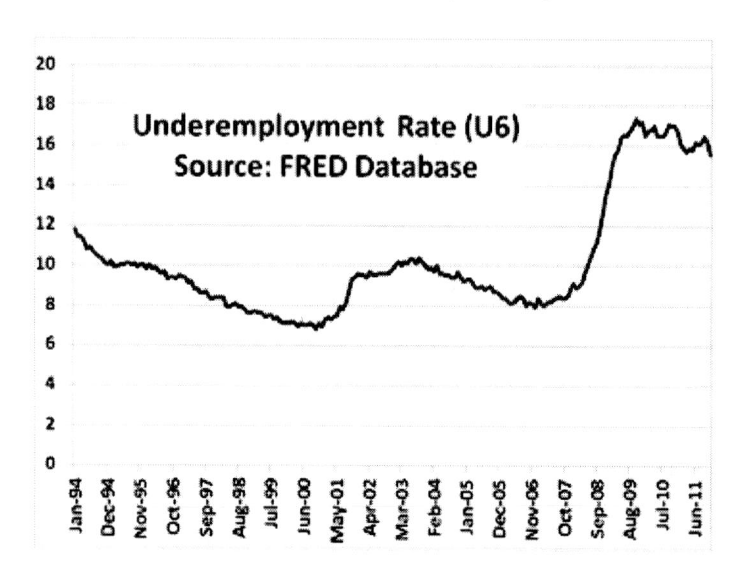

In addition to underemployment, there are also consequences for the overall economy when everybody pursues worthless degrees. Namely, the economy stops growing and starts to stagnate. Economic growth in the past averaged around 4.25% per year. There were ups and downs, but from the 1940's to the 1960's growth averaged 4.25%. However, as you see below, the long term growth rate of the US economy has been trending downwards to the point we are now growing at about half the rate we used to be. This deteriorating economic growth results in higher unemployment, lower standards of living, less income, and less of a future for everybody. There are many factors contributing to this, but one of the main ones is we no longer churn out engineers, industrialists or entrepreneurs as much as we do poets, professional activists, community organizers and social workers.

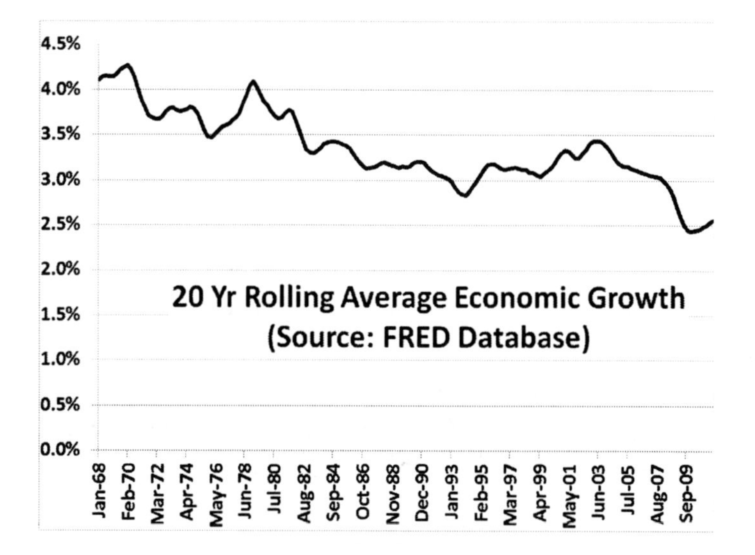

Directly related to this is precisely what we produce in the United States. If you recall, in chapter two we listed all the things people wanted and compared that list to what they were majoring in. We saw there was a huge discrepancy between what people were willing to do for work and what they ultimately wanted to purchase. With nobody majoring in computer engineering, but everybody wanting the latest smart phone or MP3 player, how is it everyone in the US has these devices? The answer is simple:

We import everything.

If you look on the back of any product you will see the majority of the stuff we like to consume in the US is made somewhere else. China, Taiwan, Indonesia, Mexico, Saudi Arabia, etc. Yes, we want the product, but we're too arrogant to dirty our hands actually making the stuff.

"What, me? Learn electrical engineering? Oh, you must be mistaken, that's beneath me. I'm an American. I'm an English major! Where's my MP3 player?"

"What, me? Major in petroleum engineering? Oh, you must be mistaken, that's beneath me. I'm an American. I'm an education major! Why is gasoline so expensive?"

The consequences are, of course, a trade deficit with the rest of the world on the order of multiple hundreds of billions of dollars, not to mention lost income, revenue and jobs that now go overseas.

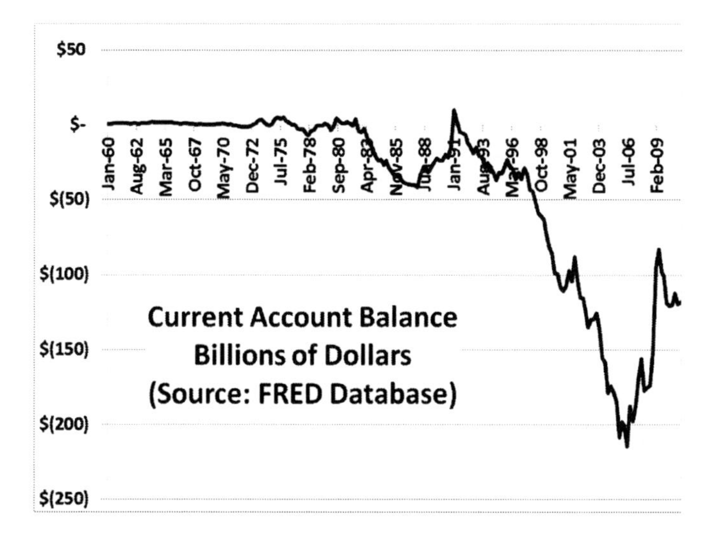

You might be asking yourself,

"Well, if we don't produce anything of value in the US and we have these perpetual trade deficits, how can we afford this?"

And that's an outstanding question!

The answer is simple – debt.

If you produce nothing, but still want to buy something, then the only way you can buy it is by going into debt. And Americans have become experts at doing this.

The federal debt is the highest it's ever been, bar WWII, currently equivalent to our GDP. That means every man, woman and child now officially owes Uncle Sam about $50,000 each. About as much as you might owe in student loans.

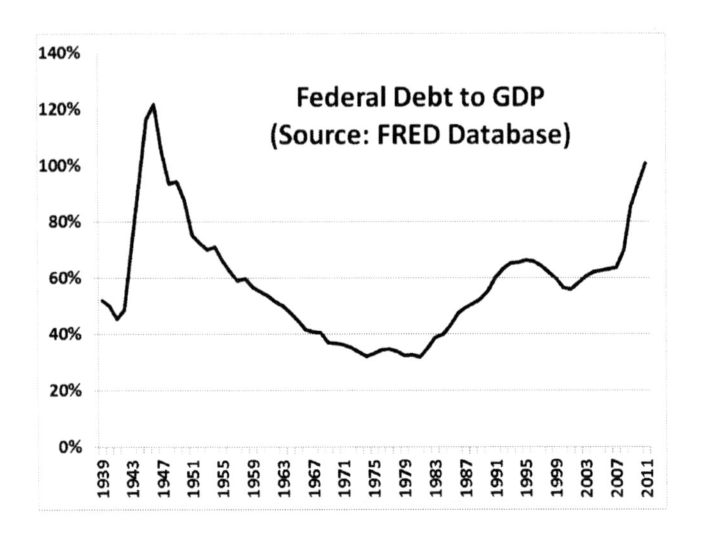

While that accounts for how our politicians spend our money, personally we're no better. You know all those neat electronic gadgets, SUV's, clothes and other items you couldn't afford but bought anyway? Or how your parents took "equity out of the house" to pay for your philosophy degree? Yeah, that adds up too. Total household debts (mortgages, credit cards, auto loans, student loans, etc.) now add up to 90% GDP (though down from a 100% at its peak).

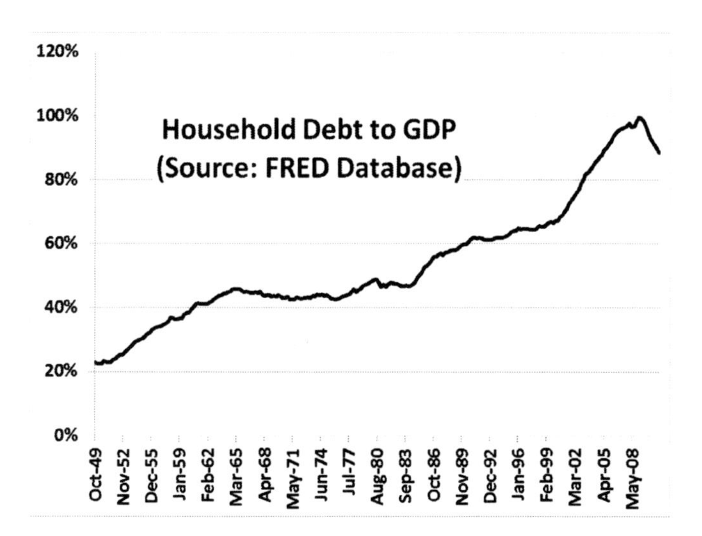

In short, the US is in its worst fiscal shape since the Civil War. This has been caused by many things, but again, 70% of people majoring in non-productive fields with non-productive jobs, is one of the primary causes. To get out of this morass and enjoy the benefits of economic growth and production, we need to major in and pursue fields of study that are practical and result in the production of goods and services people want. Or to quote a professor I knew:

"We all can't major in education and become teachers because even the liberals wouldn't have organic moose cheese and hybrid cars simply because there would be nobody around to produce the organic moose cheese and hybrid cars."

Your Moral Responsibility to Yourself

Altruism aside, there is a more important reason to choose the right major.

You.

It's nice and kind to think about society and do charitable things, but the single best thing a person can do for society is simply support themselves and enjoy life. And though, no doubt, there's been a ton of propaganda rammed down your throat to be selfless and share and think of others, there's nothing wrong with putting yourself first and making sure you have an enjoyable, successful life.

The most obvious benefit to you for choosing the right degree is the financial benefits that come along with it. In majoring in a good field you increase your earnings potential, begetting a bevy of financial benefits. Most notable is the amount of wealth you can accumulate. With high incomes and increased wealth, you can go and enjoy a better life. You can afford better food, live in a better neighborhood, drive a nicer car, and not have to go into debt to do it. You can send your kids to private schools, get them better educations, and ensure a better future for them. You can also retire earlier, travel more, and just have more leisure time in general.

Nice as the benefits of wealth are, you'll also avoid a lot of unnecessary pain and grief. Most notably you'll avoid poverty. Poverty is not fun. Most people do not know what it's like to grow up genuinely poor, but if you have, it makes life miserable. You need to worry about the basic necessities such as food, clothing and shelter. You have to sacrifice just to make ends meet. You can't go out and party with your friends, and consequently your social life suffers. You can't afford health insurance. You probably drive without auto insurance. And you can't "fly off to Europe" or "vacation in Mexico" like all your buddies do. But it's not just the economic costs of being poor, there's also an inordinate amount of psychological costs.

Unless you've lived it, the psychological stress from living in poverty is indescribable. You worry when your next paycheck is going to come in. You worry about not being able to save up for retirement. You try your best to get out of poverty, but it's out of your control, further pressing you into a helpless depression. You worry about losing your job. And sometimes you actually lose your job. Additionally, the stress doesn't go away. It's constantly there, always at the forefront of your mind. You wake up worrying about it and go to bed worrying about it. It is no shock that immigrants from poorer, foreign countries who have experienced this pain, slave away and pursue STEM degrees simply because they never want to experience poverty again. You don't have to experience this pain. You just need to major in the right degree.

Also related to stress, or the lack thereof, are some fringe benefits that come with having wealth. In having stable finances and adequate income you are likely to have better health. You probably have lower blood pressure. You have better eating habits because you can afford higher quality food. And because of your higher wages you can afford more leisure time, allowing you to work out and exercise regularly. Another fringe benefit of wealth is your family life is likely to be less problematic. Less divorce, less marital strife and your kids are less likely to commit crime or become problem children in school. Talk to anybody with stress related health problems or who is going through divorce and ask them if they'd trade it in for having to major in a tough subject for four years. I guarantee every one of them would opt to get their PhD in Computer Engineering.

The final reason you owe it to yourself to major in the right field is that in the long run it really is easier to major in a tough subject. Sure, majoring in philosophy is easier and you could probably drink your way through it (a friend of mine did). And, sure, majoring in communications would allow you a better collegiate social life than your average computer programming student. But after the four years of partying is over, the real world comes crashing down on you, and it doesn't stop. It is here the four years of grueling work earning yourself an engineering degree makes life easier and four years of goofing off earning yourself an English degree makes life hell. You get to worry about finding a job, while your engineering-majoring buddy has stable employment. You get to worry about paying back student loans, while your neurosurgeon friend has his loans paid off in his first year of practice. You get to wander the wilderness of the labor market for decades, maybe never finding stable, long term employment, while your pharmacist buddy has an immediate career. Do not be fooled by how “easy” it is to get a worthless degree. Because, while it may be easy to get it, it’s the hell it wreaks on you thereafter that makes it more difficult than the most rigorous STEM degree.

CHAPTER 9
PARTING ADVICE

In all of my seminars and classes, I usually end with a "hodge podge" of general advice. Often these bits of wisdom prove more practical and helpful than the whole seminar or class. Realize these bits of advice do not come from a chart or research, but rather real world experience. I, along with hundreds of other people, have gone down the road you are about to take and it behooves you to listen to what we're saying because we are trying to make your lives easier and better than ours. We want you to avoid our mistakes, improve upon our successes, and capitalize on our experiences.

"You really can't make any money until you're 40."
– The Great Majah Rushie

Whether you realize it or not you are a victim of your generation. The reason why is your generation, as well as the youth from previous generations, has ruined the reputation of "youths." You could be the smartest, most intelligent and gifted actuary, but if you're 23 most people are just going to lump you in with the rest of the 23 year olds. The 23 year olds that are drinking, goofing off, and are incapable of showing up to work on time. This means you are the eagle that is surrounded by turkeys and you cannot soar. But, you do have two ways you can approach this problem.

One, goof off and have fun. Since nobody is taking you seriously, just go out and have fun and avail yourself of the benefits of the bad reputation other 23 year olds have given you. This doesn't mean you don't try to start a career or that you show up to work late all the time, but you certainly don't volunteer to work weekends or commit yourself 100% to your employer. Realize at that age there really aren't going to be any career opportunities for you. There will, however, be tons of social opportunities.

Two, just commit yourself to getting a doctorate in one fell swoop. Since there are no employment opportunities, at least until you're 30, your time is better spent getting a degree that is nearly guaranteed to give you a job. And not just any ole job, but a job that will be challenging and rewarding. Remember though, you're in no rush. Nobody is going to take you seriously until you're at least 30. So if you start college at 18, you have 12 years to complete an 8 year degree. It should make getting your doctorate a lot easier, as well as grant you adequate time for a social life.

If I Were To Do It All Over

On a related note, since you really can't make any decent money until you're 40, what do you do in the meantime? Well there is one place that will take you very seriously and they will be more than happy to give you very serious work – the military.

If were to do it all over again, this is the route I would have taken. The reasons are many and compelling.

First, since nobody is going to take you seriously until you're 40, that means you'll be working in the military to the magical age of 38. Why is 38 magical? Because if you enter the military at 18 and stick with it for 20 years you will earn a lifelong pension. It may not be much, but it makes the remaining half of your life a lot easier.

Second, there are some incredible fringe benefits to the military. You have free food, clothing and shelter. You have free medical and dental care. You have training programs in the military that teach you practical skills that will help you find employment in civilian life. And, one of the best fringe benefits is they'll pay for your education.

Third, the military will give you more responsibility and more interesting work than the average civilian employer will at the age of 22. There is nothing more boring than sitting in a cubicle doing data entry as you are euphemistically called an "analyst." There is nothing more boring than sitting in a sales meeting looking at some charlatan with a marketing degree go over boring sales charts. There is, however, a lot more interesting work setting up computer networks in the field or learning how to repair a tank. Of course, the work can get a bit too interesting when you start getting shot at and IED's blow up around you, but the rewards of joining the military outweigh these risks in my opinion.

Enjoy College

Continuing on the "take your time" theme, realize you are in no rush to graduate. Not only because nobody is going to hire you for a serious position at 22, but because college, if rushed, can go from something that should be enjoyable to a hellish nightmare. A lot of you want to work hard, be the best you can be, and get into that work force and make your millions. That was me. I graduated six months early, worked full time, had three internships under my belt, didn't graduate with a dime of debt, but it was the worst three years of my life.

Meanwhile, my buddy Tom took seven years to graduate and ended up landing a higher paying job. More importantly, he got to enjoy his college experience. He got a full night's rest most nights. He went out more and partied more. He drank more. He vacationed and road-tripped more. He also chased a lot more girls (even caught a couple). In the end, I was the foolish one. All I did was waste three years of my youth. Tom was smart and enjoyed seven. Don't rush your college experience. Take it easy and enjoy it. Your career won't start without you.

Quit Right Now If You Are Majoring in a Worthless Degree

It's that simple. Quit right now. Realize you've already wasted a lot of time and money, there's no reason to continue wasting any more. However, also realize it's not like you wasted all of your college education. Usually, the first two years of college are completing prerequisites that will apply to any other degree. In the meantime, take a break from college, find some work, and take your time figuring out what worthwhile major you would like to pursue. You'd be amazed how two years in the real world will help you figure out what you should do.

Take Time Off to Work

Do not go into debt if you can avoid it. It's worthwhile to take time off from college to work up some money. If you get a decent paying job while you're in college, take the job, work it for all the cash it's worth, then return to school. Just make sure you return to school.

This is Good Debt

While it would be ideal to avoid debt altogether, understand there are good reasons to go into debt, and college is one of them. Assuming you are pursuing a worthwhile degree, do not worry about your debt load. The reason why is it is an investment, you're not frivolously spending it on a car you can't afford or clothes you don't need. I've seen a lot of students worry and fret about their debt load unnecessarily. Stop worrying. You only need to worry if the title of your degree starts with a "B.A."

Two Year Degrees

You know how I said nobody takes you seriously until you're at least 30? Well, that's in the corporate world. When it comes to the trades, however, that's a different story.

If you learn a precise skill or trade, employers will immediately put you to work in that field because the trade is so valuable. It's not like you become an ASE certified mechanic and they start you off filing or fetching coffee, inevitably working your way up to "mechanic." No, they need you deployed as a mechanic immediately.

So, if you're itching to get to work and don't want to waste a lot of time on worthless prerequisites, consider your local tech college and see if there's a program there that is of interest to you. You can be working at the age of 20, debt-free, making more than your friends when they graduate two years later with their "Bachelor's in Creative Writing."

Start Your Own Business on the Side

There is only one person you can trust in this world and that is you. Employers, no matter how successful, can always lay you off or fire you for no reason whatsoever. They can close a division down, sell out to another company, or be so horribly mismanaged they go bankrupt. You have heard stories about the guy who worked at the same firm for 30 years and then all of the sudden he was "let go?"

Yeah, don't be that guy. Have a backup plan.

One of the best backup plans is to have your own business on the side. This has many advantages. First, in case you lose your job you have something to fall back on. Two, since it's your business you get to do something you enjoy. Three, if you start early enough over time it will build faster than you realize and may even eclipse your daytime job. You will then be living the dream of doing what you like for a living. For example, I started teaching ballroom dance on the side. Wasn't anything grand when I first started, but in five years I was making an extra $30,000 a year teaching. A buddy of mine is really good with carpentry. He was making an extra $40,000 a year working on various projects. Another buddy of mine likes guns. He got his certification to teach carry-conceal and firearm safety classes and makes about $20,000.

Of course, don't be a moron and start some stupid business that is guaranteed to lose money. The perfect example is (every year, without fail) I have some middle aged woman come into my office and want to borrow money to start a horse ranch.

Why?

"Because I've always wanted to raise horses since I was a little girl!"

Do they have any experience? No. Do they have a budget? No. Did they do any projections to realize that horses cost a lot of money and the entire industry is nothing more than a massive black-hole that wipes out people's life savings and forces millions into bankruptcy? No.

They just *"Like the horses! Yeaaaa! Pretty horsies!"*

Don't be an idiot. Start a business that will make you money right off the bat and will not deplete your life savings in start-up costs you'll never recoup.

"Progressive Credentialism"

With everybody getting college degrees, the value of the degree goes down as the market gets flooded with them. This prompts people to pursue advanced degrees to make themselves more marketable, but even master's degrees are being devalued due to the flood of them hitting the market. The logical next step is then to consider getting a doctorate in the field or getting some kind of additional accreditation or certification. You see things like the CFA, CPA or "continuing education." The problem is this results in a never ending spiral. As everybody "educations-up" or "credentials-up," it lessens the value of that credential, compelling more people to get even more advanced credentials. This creates several problems.

First, don't think this spiral hasn't gone unnoticed by savvy businesses and schools in "Big Education." Schools and companies are always rolling out new certifications and credentialed programs you can take to add to your resume. Two day "executive" programs and certifications easily costing over $5,000 are offered regularly by business schools across the country. Certifications like "Six Sigma"™ offer sexy titles like "Black Belt" and "Green Belt" for people willing to pay the billion dollars to get certified. Nearly every discipline in the business field has some inane certification or accreditation. Sadly, very few of these expensive programs or certifications teach you anything practical or helpful. They're just another way to extract money from you or your employer who is obsessed with progressive and perpetual credentialism.

Second, whereas in 1950, if you graduated with a degree in accounting, you were more or less put to work immediately as a (gasp!) accountant. Today, however, because everybody has a degree, you are more likely to start as a low-end "bookkeeper." Only if you got your CPA would you be able to do higher-level accounting, and even then, a lot of places won't hire you unless you have master's classes, additional CPE certifications and "Big Four Accounting Experience." In short, the bar keeps getting moved higher and higher to do work that is more and more basic.

This results in a lot of industries becoming so "over-credentialized" that in order to get a job it may take you four years of schooling and four more years of passing various frivolous exams and certifications. Worse still, is a lot of industries are adopting this "continuing education" philosophy where you never stop taking classes. You are forced year after year to take class after class and certification after certification. It's like college never ended.

This hoop-jumping makes some industries and professions just plain not worth it. To tell if an industry or a profession is prone to this "progressive credentialism" look at the job requirements of some of their job postings. If they have a lot of acronyms in the job description (like "must have CPA, CFP, and 20 credit hours in CPE with a CME certification), forget it. It shouldn't take ten years of schooling to incubate labor, and if it does you'll spend more time taking tests than actually working.

Avoid HR

Though they are being phased out gradually, you will inevitably run into "Human Resources," more specifically the "HR Generalist." Remember, this is the 24 year old girl who knows nothing about your background, knows nothing about your field, knows nothing about the job you're applying for, but can tell a good applicant based on the color of shoes they're wearing. If you are being interviewed by HR it means you have failed to secure employment by more effective methods, namely, contacting the hiring manager.

The hiring manager is the person who determines whether or not to hire somebody. This is the person you would be working for, also affectionately called, "your boss." Most people are hired, not through the HR department, but the hiring manager. A lot of times the hiring manager already has the candidate selected, but still has to post the job and go through the charade of an interviewing process to avoid claims of favoritism. A lot of times the hiring manager hates HR and appreciates somebody trying to circumvent them. Try to meet and get to know the hiring manager. Avoid HR if you can.

Look For Employment in More Stable Countries

Because of the economic problems facing the US, and in particular, the spectacular levels of debt we have, it might be in your best interests to look for employment elsewhere. Not just because other countries have better job markets than the US does, but because if you move there and become a citizen, you won't have to pay the debt previous generations have saddled you with.

Some countries to consider are Australia, New Zealand, Singapore, Hong Kong/China, Norway and even Canada. There are others, but you can research which countries are in better financial shape than the US on the internet.

Drink More, Chase More Girls, Date More Boys

When you get to college, don't necessarily aim for the perfect "4.0." Aim for the 3.9ish area of the GPA. If you have a 4.0 you need to drink more, chase more girls, or date more boys. If your credit load prevents any of this, lower your credit load to make time for these vital collegiate activities.

THE END

SPECIAL THANKS

Natasha, Sindi and Marty – Two good looking girls and…well…Marty. Thanks for the editing. If there are any typos or mistakes found, it's your guys' fault.

Craig "The Leak" Kamman – Another cunning plan, sir

My Aunt Judy, who will no doubt buy this book AND not read it.

St. Mary's and the U of MN Women's Studies Department – Thank you for the mindless pablum in your course descriptions. It made for great fodder for the book.

Mr. Gilles – Thanks for having me talk to the kids at the U of MN and CFACT

My 7th Grade English Teacher - Still teaching English to English-speaking kids, I presume?

Prof. Caliendo and Prof. Maitland – The only professors that earned their keep

All the Junior, Aspiring, Deputy, Official and Otherwise Economists at Cappy Cap

CPSIA information can be obtained at www.ICGtesting.com
Printed in the USA
LVOW12s1145010714

392518LV00001B/46/P